FRANCE

The East

TIME-LIFE BOOKS/AMSTERDAM

COOKERY AROUND THE WORLD
FRANCE The East

AMANDINE DITTA BIEGI

Food photography: Michael Brauner

English Channel

Belgium

Nord-Pas de Calais

Luxem-burg

Germany

Upper Normandy

Picardy

Lower Normandy

Paris

Ile de France

Lorraine

Alsace

Champagne-Ardenne

Brittany

Centre

Pays de la Loire

Burgundy

Franche Comté

Switzerland

Atlantic

Poitou-Charentes

Limousin

Auvergne

Rhône (Lyonnais)

Ain (Bresse)

Upper Savoy

Rhône-Alpes

Savoy

Aquitaine

Isère (Dauphiné)

Italy

Midi-Pyrénées

Languedoc-Roussillon

Provence-Alpes-Côte d'Azur

Corsica

Spain

Mediterranean

N

0   50   100   150 KM

Le Vieux Lyon

MENU

CONTENTS

France: The East – A Region of Rural Pleasures ———— 7

A Traditional Culinary Heritage ———————— 9

  Alsace ————————————————— 10

  Lorraine ————————————————— 12

  Champagne-Ardenne and Burgundy ——————— 14

  Franche-Comté ———————————————— 16

  Bresse and Savoy ——————————————— 18

  Dauphiné and Lyonnais ———————————— 20

  Auvergne —————————————————— 22

  Limousin —————————————————— 24

Recipes ——————————————————— 27

  Cocktail Nibbles and Snacks —————————— 27

  Hors d'œuvre ————————————————— 37

  Fish ———————————————————— 55

  Meat ———————————————————— 67

  Game and Poultry ——————————————— 85

  Vegetables ————————————————— 103

  Cheese ——————————————————— 113

  Desserts —————————————————— 121

Suggested Menus ———————————————— 138

Glossary ——————————————————— 140

Index ————————————————————— 142

Acknowledgements and Picture Credits ——————— 144

Note on Map:
The map divisions show the modern administrative regions of France. Within the Rhône-Alpes region the names of the old provinces—by which the culinary regions of this part of France are best known—appear in brackets under the names of the current *départements*. The former province of Lyonnais used to extend over the border of what is now Burgundy, while the old province of Dauphiné is now in the northern part of present-day Provence-Alpes-Côte d'Azur.

FRANCE: THE EAST A REGION OF RURAL PLEASURES

astern France and the Massif Central are regions with a varied and many-faceted landscape. A good way to explore them would be to take a long and leisurely round trip, perhaps starting with the idyllic little wine-producing villages of Alsace, Burgundy and Champagne, then travelling eastwards to the French Jura in Franche-Comté and the awe-inspiring white mountains of Savoie. From there, the route could meander

through Dauphiné and Bresse into Lyon, a city famous for its love of fine food, and finally westwards to the rugged heights of the Auvergne and the dense forests of Limousin.

In the small towns and villages of these regions, countless old farmhouses, former mills and romantically situated châteaux have been adapted to provide *chambres et tables d'hôte* for visitors. In these, guests can live with a host family under one roof and get to know the region, the people and local culinary traditions far better than would be possible if they stayed in a hotel. Through their own first-hand experience, they can quickly discover the true French way of life.

On a typical day the guest might awake in the morning to the aroma of fresh croissants and baguettes, which are served with milky coffee and home-made jam. Breakfast is frugal, in order not to spoil the appetite for lunch. On working days the French midday meal consists of a starter and a main course, followed by cheese and dessert. Dinner and Sunday lunch have an extra course. No French meal is complete without a glass of wine with the food, and a coffee to finish.

For most French people, cooking is a pleasure not a chore. Even women with full-time jobs will spend hours lovingly preparing food for friends and family, even if only at the weekend. Large Sunday lunches and special meals to celebrate particular festivals are part of the culinary tradition in most families, with everyone lending a hand in the preparations. Ingredients can be bought fresh from the market every day, including Sunday mornings.

The purpose of this book is to take you on a gastronomic voyage through eastern France and the Massif Central. The first chapter describes in words and pictures the beauties of the landscape and the cultural and historic monuments of the various regions, and it introduces some of the mouth-watering local foods and wines.

The rest of the chapters form the recipe section, and are arranged in the traditional order in which dishes are served in France. This section includes the region's most famous specialities, from small cocktail snacks to desserts. A special feature of the book is a chapter devoted to cheese recipes. All the dishes are explained step by step and illustrated with a colour photograph, enabling even novice cooks to re-create them with ease; more complicated techniques are described in detail with clear illustrations.

Complementing the recipes wherever possible are interesting variations, useful hints and information, and recommendations for suitable wines to drink with particular dishes. And to help with the never-ending question "What shall I cook today?" the recipe section ends with menu suggestions for a whole range of meals from a simple snack lunch to a slap-up feast. A glossary at the end of the book explains some important ingredients and expressions used in French cuisine.

One phrase needs no explanation and you will hear it wherever you eat in France: *bon appétit!*

A TRADITIONAL CULINARY HERITAGE

In eastern France and the Massif Central, the visitor soon feels at home. The charming countryside, with its sleepy villages and friendly inhabitants, is a far cry from the hustle and bustle of Paris or the sophisticated style of the Côte d'Azur. The best time to visit is between the end of May, when the fields and vineyards are beginning to turn green, and the end of September, when the grapes are harvested— unless, of course, the region's many winter sports and activities are more to your liking.

Discovering the cuisine of eastern France and the Massif Central is like embarking on a journey into the culinary past. In these largely rural regions, people cook as they always have done – painstakingly and with attention to quality, preparing ingredients so that they do not lose their characteristic flavours. Perhaps most importantly, no matter how simple the meal, the food is prepared with love.

The recent popularity of regional cuisine and traditional specialities is currently reflected in the success of provincial restaurants, which are flourishing while their "modern" competitors are used—mostly by younger people—as no more than somewhere to fill up at little cost.

After all, everyone looks forward to Sunday lunch *chez Mamie*, as grandmother is known in French.

It is the so-called *petit peuple*, the ordinary people, who cherish the culinary heritage of their region. Through often arduous work in the fields and vineyards, in small bakeries and cheese factories, they continue their age-old traditions.

For these independent farmers and craftsmen and women running their own small food businesses it is not a question of money, for they do not earn much. Nor is it a matter of prestige, for their rural occupations do not win them much esteem from the outside world. They take pride in their work because they love it and their products more than meet the high standards expected of French gastronomy. Such dedication is more important in maintaining a country's culinary heritage than any number of top chefs in luxury restaurants.

It matters not that a district or its products may be overshadowed by another with a greater or more famous name. Each region has its own specialities, and often it is the poorest stretch of land that has encouraged the development of a particularly imaginative and delicious cuisine.

Be prepared to be both surprised and delighted.

Alsace

Squeezed between the Vosges mountains to the west and the River Rhine and Germany to the east, Alsace is a feast for the eyes and the palate. Its appeal owes much to its varied scenery, which is dotted with fairytale castles, and to its historic towns and villages with their multitude of cultural attractions and gourmet delights.

Strasbourg, the region's dynamic capital, has a long and distinguished history. Its cathedral offers an impressive example of medieval architecture, while the former tanners' quarter, known as *Petite France*, and the canals lined with lovingly restored half-timbered houses vividly evoke the city's past. Even more picturesque is the *Petite Venise* quarter of Colmar, a busy town due south of Strasbourg. Here, small boats glide silently beneath splendid arched bridges and past gaily coloured houses.

Those who enjoy the countryside should not miss the Route de la Choucroute, or "sauerkraut road". This pleasant route runs south from Holtzheim near Strasbourg to Obenheim am Rhein, winding its way through charming scenery.

Another road well worth taking is the Alsatian wine route between Marlenheim, west of Strasbourg, and Thann, near Mulhouse, in the south. There are many romantic wine-producing towns and villages along the way, including the enchanting little medieval town of Riquewihr and the ancient city of Obernai, which was one of ten Alsatian cities to form a union under the control of the Holy Roman Emperor in the twelfth century. Near Colmar, the road leads through Kaysersberg, the birthplace of the 1952 Nobel Peace prizewinner Albert Schweitzer, which also boasts historic museums, Romanesque chapels and the ruins of medieval fortresses.

Louis XIV was so impressed by Alsace's many natural, cultural and culinary treasures that he dubbed it *pays heureux*, the fortunate land. Certainly, today's Alsatians are lucky in their cuisine, which is a blend of hearty traditional dishes and the refined creations of French master chefs. In eighteenth-century Strasbourg, for example, a certain Clause, cook to the Maréchal de Contade, "invented" *pâté de foie gras*. Other local specialities,

A musician in Colmar produces unusual sounds from an instrument of his own invention.

Including *tarte flambée* and *choucroute garnie* (sauerkraut with meat and sausages from freshly slaughtered pigs), are served in the small restaurants known as Winstuben. At one time, *choucroute garnie* was a special dish, eaten only on Sundays.

There are dozens of meat, poultry and game dishes to sample, as well as wonderful fish specialities, but Münster is the only local cheese. Every patisserie has tempting fruit tarts, doughnuts, gâteaux, Christstollen (a Christmas fruit loaf) and waffles. Kugelhopf, a sweet yeast cake, is a favourite Sunday breakfast food, especially when accompanied by a glass of Gewurztraminer, a spicy wine with a rich bouquet.

Alsatians are justifiably proud of their wines, which blend perfectly with local dishes and more refined French cuisine alike. Alsace is the only region of France where the wines bear the name of the grapes from which they are made: Riesling, Gewurztraminer, Sylvaner, Muscat, Tokay, Pinot Gris, Pinot Blanc and Pinot Noir, which is sometimes called Klevner. The finest grape varieties are used in the production of the champagne-style Crémant d'Alsace. Beer is also prominent in Alsace, with half of France's production being brewed in the region. And to round off a perfect meal, one of the 40 varieties of schnapps or liqueurs made from local fruit, berries or roots is sure to please.

Festivals

With more than 36 food festivals in the year, there is always something to celebrate in Alsace. There are feasts in honour of all types of food including white turnips, onions, hops, beer, sugar, nuts, *pâté en croûte* (meat pies), cheese and sauerkraut, as well as, naturally, many wine festivals.

Flower-decked half-timbered houses in the little town of Riquewihr.

Old signs, like these in Strasbourg, can be seen hanging over inns and shops throughout Alsace.

Lorraine

The quiet province of Lorraine is markedly different from its neighbours, Alsace to the east and Champagne to the west. The architecture is plain and there is little traffic on the roads. The region holds many delights for walkers, however. Lorraine can be reached on foot from Alsace over the Col de la Schlucht pass, which takes in some splendid panoramic views over the dark green fir trees of the Vosges mountains. Westward from the Vosges, the land gently flattens across Lorraine into the softly undulating countryside of Champagne.

Spa towns such as Amnéville, Bains-les-Bains, Contrexéville, Plombières and Vittel have been famous for centuries for their luxury, elegance and tranquil rural settings. Anyone who likes water, woodland and the changing colours of nature will find much to appreciate. In the wooded hills near Saulnois, between the university towns of Metz and Nancy, there are monuments, bird sanctuaries and fish-filled lakes. The Route du Poisson, or "fish road", links the ponds of Lorraine's many fish farms, and there is plenty of opportunity along the way to sample some of the good, plain freshwater fish dishes which are typical of the region.

Lorraine's capital, Metz, is home to many cultural treasures, including the great cathedral of St-Etienne, which stands on a flat-topped hill overlooking the city's picturesque roof tops. At Nancy, music lovers can enjoy a year-round programme of events, while art enthusiasts will find works by many Art Nouveau artists exhibited at the École

de Nancy Museum. Orange-scented boiled sweets called bergamottes are a speciality of the city and make an appropriate souvenir.

Over the years, Lorraine's cooks have been spurred on to achieve great heights by the proximity of Alsace and Burgundy, two neighbouring regions which are famed for their fine cuisine. While home cooking retains its traditional simplicity, old recipes have been successfully refined with touches of grande cuisine. The most noteworthy traditional dishes are *potée* (meat hotpot), quiche lorraine (bacon quiche) and sucking pig. The most typical cheese of the region is the pungent Münster-Géromé.

Lorraine is rich in food resources. The rivers and ponds provide plentiful trout, perch, pike, carp, crayfish and frogs, which are transformed into wonderful dishes—often through the

Catholic emblems, like this Madonna and Child, can be seen in many gardens in Lorraine.

addition of cream and wine. Soft fruits—raspberries, red- and blackcurrants, cherries, plums and bilberries—grow abundantly in Lorraine. The star fruit of the region is the golden-yellow mirabelle plum, which is unique in that it carries an official certificate of quality, the AOC (Appellation d'Origine Contrôlée). The first mirabelle trees were planted at the command of King René as long ago as the fifteenth century, and the area around Lunéville, southeast of Nancy, is particularly famous for them.

Lunéville is also famous for a rum-soaked yeast cake called *baba au rhum*. Tradition has it that the cake was invented by Stanislas Leszczynski, a former Polish king and father-in-law to King Louis XV who set up residence in the Château de Lunéville. Today *Baba au rhum* is extremely popular throughout Lorraine, as are madeleines, little scallop-shaped lemon tea cakes.

As one might expect in a region of spa towns, Lorraine is the source of well-known mineral waters, notably Vittel and Contrexéville. Beer is brewed at Champigneulles near Nancy and some wine, mostly a pale rosé known as *vin gris*, is produced along the Moselle river and in the area around Toul. Another local speciality is *aux-de-vie de mirabelle*, a potent spirit made from the famous plums.

Festivals

A big annual festival in honour of the little round mirabelles is held in Metz in late August/early September. In mid-June a salt festival is held at Marsal, where at other times of the year visitors can see the fascinating four-thousand-year-old story of salt at the town's unique Maison du Sel museum.

The people of Lorraine are open and friendly. The basque beret is typical headgear in this region, as it is throughout France.

Handsome half-timbered houses line the narrow streets of the old town of Troyes in Champagne.

Champagne-Ardenne

The Champagne-Ardenne region extends south from the Belgian border to the source of the river Marne. It is best explored in a leisurely fashion, travelling along picturesque roads which wind their way from north to south through the wooded Ardenne hills, past vineyards, huge cornfields and villages bright with flowers.

Wine buffs should take the Champagne route which leads through the three great Champagne-producing areas. These lie to the south of Epernay, along the Vallée de la Marne, and in the Montagne de Reims. It is well worth visiting the extensive tunnels and cellars carved into the underlying chalk of the region. Here, several million bottles of champagne are stored and left to mature.

The city of Reims holds many attractions, notably the gothic cathedral with its truncated tower, which was once the coronation seat of the kings of France. Also of interest are the Palais du Tau, the former archbishop's palace, and an imposing Roman arch built in the third century.

The cuisine of Champagne-Ardenne is delicious and varied. Fish is often served in a sauce made with red wine from Bouzy in the Montagne de Reims, and the addition of a boiling fowl gives the *potée* (meat hotpot) its distinctive flavour. The best-known cheeses are the slightly sour *chaource*, which has a fresh white rind, and tangy *Langres*, from the town of the same name, which has an orange rind. *Chaource, gâteau mollet* (iced brioche) and *biscuits roses de Reims* (pink sponge cakes with icing) are all eaten accompanied by champagne.

Festivals

Under the auspices of the Yehudi Menuhin Foundation, Reims offers music lovers an annual feast of 120 concerts. Every third year, between late September and early October, Charleville-Mézières plays host to the world puppet festival.

Burgundy

The grape varieties from which the *grands crus* (great wines) of Burgundy are produced—Pinot Noir, Gamay, Chardonnay, Aligoté and Sauvignon—grow along a narrow north-to-south strip of well-situated fertile soil. The 40-kilometre route from Dijon to

Beaune is lined with glorious vineyards and world-famous wine villages, including Gevrey-Chambertin, Nuits-St-George and Vougeot.

The picture-book countryside is dotted with châteaux and abbeys, such as the Cistercian Cîteaux. Northeast of Dijon the river Seine rises in a richly wooded area blessed with lakes full of fish. To the south, white Charolais cattle graze in the green meadows.

Beaune, a town which owes its wealth to the grape, is home to the Hôtel-Dieu, a charity hospital which is a masterpiece of Flemish-Burgundian architecture. Dijon, Burgundy's capital, is popular with gourmets and visitors interested in history. It is world-famous for its mustard, while *cassissines de Dijon* (blackcurrant sweets) are a popular gift to take home for friends and family.

Burgundian cuisine is a harmonious blend of food and wine. Specialities include *escargots* (vineyard snails), *jambon persillé* (boiled ham in parsley aspic) and *boeuf bourguignon* (beef in red wine). Fish is served with white or red wine sauces. Custard tarts and local cheeses, such as *Époisses* (matured in local brandy), *Montrachet* (wrapped in chestnut leaves), creamy *Cîteaux* (made by Cistercian monks) and *Charolais* round off the meal.

Matching the food to perfection are the great Burgundian wines of Chablis, the Côte de Nuits, (Gevrey-Chambertin, Vougeot), Côte Chalonnaise (Rully, Mercurey, Givry), Côte de Beaune (Montrachet, Puligny-Montrachet), and Mâconnais (Pouilly-Fuissé). The region is also noted for Kir, an aperitif of dry white burgundy wine flavoured with cassis, which is named after a mayor of Dijon said to have invented it.

Festivals

The arrival of barrel organs and hurdy-gurdies from all over Europe in late September transforms Dijon into a vast open-air museum for the duration of the festival of mechanical music. At the beginning of November, the city hosts France's most famous food festival, the international gastronomic fair, as it has done since 1921.

Burgundy is criss-crossed by canals, making it possible to explore the region by houseboat.

Visitors are welcome to sample the wine in the cellars of Champagne and Burgundy.

Montbéliard cows supply the milk for making Franche-Comté's delicious cheeses.

Franche-Comté

Mountainous Franche-Comté stretches along the border with Switzerland, from the Jura Massif to Lake Geneva. Much of the region is covered in pine forest, interspersed with bright green meadows and brilliant blue lakes. The trees stretch up to 45 metres high, while their trunks can reach 1.3 metres in diameter. The shady forest floor is rich in wonderful mushrooms, such as morels and chanterelles.

One of the best ways to see the region is to follow the "Comté cheese road" from Saint-Hippolyte, in the northeast, to Montfleur, near Bourg. Along the way you can visit one of the many small cheese factories, known as *fruitières*, to watch the making of the local hard cheese, *vrai Comté*, which is also on display at the Maison du Comté at Poligny, near Arbois. As long ago as the twelfth century alpine dairies were making this distinctive cheese with its pea-size holes and inimitable nutty flavour. Each cheese measures 70 cm across, weighs 48 kg, and uses at least 500 litres of milk from the local Montbéliard cows.

The region's wine route leads from Salins-les-Bains to Saint-Amour, passing through a series of wine-producing villages that nestle in the sunny foothills of the Jura. Vineyards cover the slopes of the chalk plateau known as Revermont or *Bon Pays* (good country). Arbois has a wine and wine-making museum, which makes a special exhibit of the four wines from the region to carry an Appellation d'Origine Contrôlée (AOC): Arbois, Château-Chalon, Côtes du Jura and l'Étoile. The museum also has a feature on Louis Pasteur, who once lived in the town. His experiments with the fermentation of alcohol did much to help the local wine industry.

With its plentiful streams, rivers, ponds and more than 80 lakes, Franche-Comté is an angler's paradise. Each river has its own varieties: barbel in the Ognon, trout and tench in the Ain, carp in the Saône and char in the Loue. Fish-lovers should take the *Route des Mille Étangs*, "road of a thousand fishponds", from the Vosges mountains to the River Saône, passing through the peaceful thermal spa town of Luxeuil-les-Bains in the north.

The *Route horlogère franco-suisse*, "Franco-Swiss clockmakers' route",

goes from Besançon to Neuchâtel in Switzerland. Besançon, the capital of Franche-Comté, is still an important clockmaking centre. Caramels are another speciality. One of the city's most ancient districts is the Quartier Battant, where the winemakers, known locally as *bousbots,* once lived.

Butter, cream, cheese and smoked meats are typical ingredients of Franche-Comté cuisine. Among the products of the farmers' smokehouses are *Jésus de Morteau,* a plump pork sausage on a skewer, *brési,* dried beef, and Luxeuil ham. As well as *Comté,* the region is famed for its *Emmental grand cru,* a delicately flavoured blue cheese, *Septmoncel,* soft *cancoillotte,* a kind of small Vacherin called *Mont d'or,* and *Morbier* made from untreated milk and marked with a black stripe.

Simple, rustic desserts like *galette briochée de Montbéliard* and *galette de goumeau*—both kinds of custard tart—are delicious accompanied by Jura wines. Franche-Comté wines are excellent for laying down. The rosés and reds can be kept for about ten years, and the white Chardonnays up to fifty years. *Vin de paille,* "straw wine", is made from grapes dried on straw mats before pressing and will keep for several dozen years, while the yellow oak-aged *vin jaune,* produced exclusively from the Savagnin grape, will keep for up to a hundred years. In *Crémant* the region has an excellent sparkling wine, either white or rosé.

Festivals

At Pesmes, the banks of the river are illuminated each July for the *Fête de l'Ognon.* In early September, the *Festival de Musique de Besançon Franche-Comté* is held in Besançon and ten other towns in the region.

Still small at this point, the River Loue flows through the picturesque little town of Ornans.

Men of Bresse enjoy a conversation over a glass or two of local wine.

Bresse

Between the foothills of the Jura in the east and the flatlands of the River Saône in the west lies the gentle wooded region of Bresse, famous for its corn and its chickens. The countryside is characterized by closely packed rows of trees, hedges and stands of willow, among which lie long, flat-roofed farmhouses typical of the area. Built from clay or brick, many still have the huge, old-fashioned *cheminée sarrasine*, "Saracen chimney", with an open flue over a fire in the centre of the living room.

Dry or drying corncobs can usually be seen hanging from the farmhouse balconies. These provide nourishment for both the chickens and the local people, who owe their nickname *ventres jaunes*—"yellow bellies"—to the large stocks of golden corn which they consume. As if aware of their reputation, the chickens strut proudly around the fields of those farmers who are licensed to raise them.

Bourg, capital of the *département* of Ain, is the most important city of the region and it is well worth a detour to see its old town. Also worth visiting is the late Gothic church at Brou with its three mausoleums, one of France's architectural treasures. The bird sanctuary of Villars-les-Dombes is a good starting point for a tour around the thousand little fish-breeding ponds of the Dombes Plateau, an area as famous for its fish specialities as its unspoilt countryside.

Bresse cuisine centres on traditional chicken dishes. The region is also noted for its *Bresse bleu*, a mild blue cheese, and wines such as Seyssel and Roussette from the Bugey area. *Bonbons de chocolat de Bourg-en-Bresse* are a popular sweetmeat.

Festivals

Several places in Bresse, including Montrevel-en-Bresse, Pont-de-Vaux and Bourg-en-Bresse, stage annual poultry competitions—*Concours de volailles*—on the third Saturday in December. After the prizegiving for the best birds, the celebrations usually continue with folk music and dancing.

Savoy

From the flat country of Bresse to the west, the landscape of Savoy climbs eastwards to the highest point in

Europe—the 4,807-metre Mont Blanc. This is a region of many different faces. In summer, the green mountains offer leisurely walks or energetic hikes with splendid views of steeply rising peaks. The clear blue lakes are perfect for water sports such as swimming, diving, water-skiing and sailing, while rushing white water rivers are just right for canoeing. In winter, the snow-covered mountains offer every imaginable kind of winter sport.

In short, Savoy has something to suit every taste, from a peaceful country rest or relaxing cure at a spa such as Aix-les-Bains, to a stay amid the hustle and bustle of Chambéry, Annecy or the Olympic town of Albertville. Ancient castles, fortresses and opulent baroque churches can be admired in many towns and villages. And Chambéry's Musée des Beaux Arts, with its stunning modern art collection, should not be missed.

The infinitely varied countryside of Savoy provides generously for the table. Cheeses such as deeply fissured *Beaufort*, creamy-flavoured *Reblochon* and nutty-tasting *Tomme de Savoie* are still produced in alpine huts; fish is freshly caught in the clear waters of the lakes and rivers; and the forests supply berries, mushrooms, and delicious honey flavoured with the delicate fragrance of alpine flowers.

The dry white and fruity red wines are well worth sampling. Évian and Thonon mineral waters are bottled from local springs. For vermouth-lovers, Chambéry has been distilling its own version since 1932, and its truffles will delight the sweet-toothed.

Festivals

In August, Aix-les-Bains celebrates a flower festival with fireworks. Mid-August sees a wine-and-alpine festival at Notre-Dame de Bellecombe.

Peace and relaxation can be found on Lac de Tignes near Val d'Isère.

Mountain farmers still do much of the work by hand to bring in the hay in the western Alps near Grenoble.

Dauphiné

With a patchwork of varied landscapes and people of diverse characters, Dauphiné is something of a microcosm of France. The region extends from the plains of the Rhône valley to the peaks and deep gorges of the Oisan Massif east of Grenoble. One of the best ways to see the magnificent scenery is to take a trip on a cable car or the vertiginous mountain railway.

Mountain-encircled Grenoble should also be seen from on high: the view from the Bastille is quite exceptional. Grenoble hosted the 1968 Winter Olympics and has much of interest for the visitor, including the Musée Dauphinois, a museum of local history, and a collection of paintings by Hébert at the museum bearing his name.

Set amid barren mountains, the Monastère de la Grande Chartreuse is shrouded in as much mystery as the recipe for its famous liqueur. At any one time, only three monks know the formula, which is said to include 130 herbs. Yellow and green chartreuse are now distilled under the monks' supervision at Voiron, near Grenoble, where the cellars are open to visitors.

The nearby town of Saint-Marcellin makes a fine, soft cow's milk cheese and has a cheese museum. Cheese dishes in Dauphiné cuisine include *gratin dauphinois* (sliced potatoes baked in cream) and, reflecting the influence of neighbouring Italy, ravioli stuffed with ewe's milk cheese.

Walnuts are an important local crop, especially northwest of Grenoble around Morain. Grenoble itself is famous for its rich walnut cake, and walnut liqueur is another speciality of the area. Home-made aperitifs, like nut wine, are among the more unusual regional specialities. These are made with the red and white wines from the vineyards of Les Crozes Hermitages.

Festivals

There are more than 200 festivals in the region, including bread festivals at Montferrat in June and at Villar d'Arène in July. At the international folklore festival, also in July, you can feast on spit-roasted meat.

Lyonnais

South of Burgundy, Lyonnais is a small province with a big reputation. Its beautiful mountains can be explored on foot or on horseback, while a boat trip along the Saône takes you past romantic Beaujolais villages and the colourful house facades along the Quai

de Saône in the city of Lyon. The peninsula at the confluence of the Rhône and Saône offers a fine view of Lyon's old town, Vieux Lyon, with the Basilique de Fourvière looming over it. Inside are delightful little medieval houses with Gothic inner courtyards. The city's bistros, known locally as *bouchons*, serve typical snacks called *mâchons* from 9.00 a.m.

A visit to Lyon should include a meal prepared by one of the *mères*—women cooks who have dominated the city's culinary activities since the French Revolution. Some of today's top chefs learnt their trade from these female chefs, and what is now known as *grande cuisine* has its roots in their kitchens. Today, there are still disciples of the traditional *mères* who assess what their customers "ought to eat" and then take pleasure in feeding them. In this gastronomic capital,

people like to eat—and eat a lot. Among the traditional dishes are *salade lyonnaise*, *cervelle de canut* (curd cheese with herbs), and chicken in cream sauce.

Wine flows so freely in these parts it is sometimes referred to as the "third river" after the Rhône and the Saône. The region has no fewer than nine *crus*, or top quality wines, which are famous throughout the world: Saint-Amour, Juliénas, Chénas, Moulin-à-Vent, Fleurie, Chiroubles, Morgon, Régnié and Brouilly. Visitors would do well to take a case home with them.

Festivals

In addition to almost weekly culinary festivals held across the region, the most famous wine festivals are the Fêtes des Crus de Beaujolais at Chiroubles in April and the Beaujolais Nouveau celebrations in November.

A trompe l'œil mural on the side of a building in Lyon.

Flowers, fresh fruit and vegetables on sale at the market on Quai Saint-Antoine in Lyon.

Auvergne

Set in the heart of France, the
Auvergne is a vast stretch of unspoilt
countryside. Here, the scenery
alternates between gigantic volcanoes,
rugged gorges and beautiful glacier
valleys with clear, calm lakes, rushing
rivers and pure springs.

More than a quarter of the landscape
is the result of volcanic activity. The
most ancient volcanoes, such as Cantal
and Mont Dore, have been extinct for
millions of years, but the volcanic chain
of Les Puys only came into being
between 6000 and 8500 years ago.
Today, the conical volcanoes are
covered with grass or woodland and the
craters are filled with icy water that is
well-stocked with carp and char. At Le
Puy-en-Velay, the Chapelle Saint-Michel
d'Aiguilhe (*above*) is set on a spike of
volcanic rock. With Notre-Dame de
France, a huge statue of the Virgin

Mary, it towers over a sea of houses
and rooftops.

The most impressive view of the
volcanoes is from above, which the
more adventurous visitor can achieve
by air balloon, para-glider or hang-
glider. Indeed, for those who like
adventure sports the region is a
paradise. In the summer you can shoot
white water rapids by canoe, raft, or in
a group trip by rubber dinghy. In winter
you can try dog-sledding and some
extremely challenging ski runs. The
less energetic might prefer to visit the
world-famous spa resort of Vichy.

The region's main river, the Allier, is
Western Europe's largest salmon river.
Every winter the salmon swim some
900 kilometres upstream along the
Loire and then the Allier to lay their
eggs in the place where they
themselves hatched five years earlier.

One road recommended to travellers
runs across the Auvergne from west to

east, past fortresses and châteaux which bring the history of France to life. Many of the châteaux, such as La Palice, are now lived in once again; others house exhibitions, let rooms to visitors, or, like Murol, provide venues for theatrical shows.

The people of the Auvergne are particularly gifted with manual skills. Along the *Route des métiers*, the "craft road", which runs through the Livradois-Forez Nature Park, castles, museums and private houses provide opportunities to learn about the history and techniques of traditional crafts. Exquisite lacework is on display in the lacemakers' house at Brioude and the Musée Crozatier in Le Puy. Handmade pillow lace is a popular souvenir of the region.

Just as Lyon owes its fame for fine cuisine to its *mères*, so the Auvergne has its *menettes* to thank for its culinary style. The *menettes* were young women of the Order of the Blessed Saint Agnes who worked for noble families. The older girls initiated the younger ones into the mysteries of cookery. Today, both home and professional cooks follow recipes handed down by the *menettes*.

Although Charolais and Salers cattle as well as excellent poultry are raised in the Auvergne region, it is pork, fondly known as "Monsieur le Porc", which takes pride of place on the menu. Accordingly, pig's trotter terrine is known as *Pied de Monsieur en terrine*.

Auvergne's finest vegetables are green lentils from Le Puy, which are especially good with *gigot brayaude*, slowly roasted leg of mutton. Above all, however, Auvergne cuisine is cheese cuisine. The best-known local potato specialities, *aligot* and *truffade*, are made with *Cantal* cheese. *Fourme d'Ambert* and *bleu d'Auvergne* are two buttery blue cheeses. *Saint Nectaire*, a farmhouse cheese made from cows' milk, is left to mature for two months in former wine cellars.

Saint Pourçain wine comes from the oldest vineyards in France and is served with regional specialities and cheeses. Mineral waters from the region—Vichy, Volvic, Mont-Dore and Saint-Yorre—are world famous.

Festivals

An international folklore festival takes place at Gannat in the last week in July. The streets of Aurillac are full of colourful activity during the European festival of street theatre in late August. The *Fête Roi de l'Oiseau*, the Festival of the Bird King, at Le Puy-en-Velay in mid-September, revives old customs and traditions.

Pillow lacemaking is a traditional craft in the Auvergne.

The broad Picherande plateau near the Mont Dore in the Auvergne.

Typical steep roofs in the charming town of Uzerche, known as the "pearl of Limousin".

Limousin

There was a time when lazy or disagreeable public servants were threatened with exile to Limousin, a half-forgotten region at the heart of France: *se faire limoger* meant "to be transferred for disciplinary reasons". Today, however, city-dwellers dream of having a second home there, far away from busy traffic routes. Along the country roads of Limousin there are usually more cattle than cars; time seems to stand still there.

This is a land of dense forests—oak, birch, beech, chestnut and conifer abound—and wide, lush pastures and bushy hedges. Almost everywhere can be heard the babble of streams and rivers, and with 75 lakes set amid the forests almost every angler and sailor can have their own strip of water.

Civilization did not bypass Limousin altogether, however. Among many masterpieces of Romanesque architecture are the abbey church of Beaulieu and the monastery of Mouthier-d'Ahun. The Château de Val in the Dordogne is well worth visiting, too. With its narrow, winding streets the town of Uzerche is known as "the pearl of Limousin", but it is only one pearl among many. Collonge-la-Rouge, built entirely from red sandstone, has to count among the most beautiful villages in France.

At Aubusson you can visit tapestry weaving mills, where men and women sit bent over their looms as they have done for 300 years. The best view across the town's rooftops is from the nearby cliffs. In Brive there is a lively and colourful weekly market, where it is fun to join the crowds and stroll from stall to stall. The candied fruit is particularly worth buying.

Limoges is the world-renowned centre of Limousin's enamel and porcelain industry. The finest and most artistic pieces of porcelain are on display there in the Musée National de la Ceramique Adrien-Dubouché. The best examples of enamel are to be found in the municipal museum, which also has a collection of paintings by Pierre Auguste Renoir, who was born in Limoges in 1841.

Unusually, Limoges has two old towns: the Bishop's Town, with the cathedral and episcopal palace, and the old commercial centre. In the latter, the Rue de la Boucherie (Butcher Street) has been home to generations of the same families since 1200. They built their own chapel, the Chapelle St Aurelien, which was formerly reserved exclusively for the butchers of Limoges. Inside, a statue of the Christ Child sitting on His mother's lap depicts Him clutching a kidney! A few streets away is the covered market—the "belly" of Limoges—which offers a wonderful selection of local specialities, from chestnut liqueur to *pâté de foie gras*.

It is hard to believe that only a few decades ago Limousin was so poor that the diet consisted of little more than chestnuts and walnuts. Chestnuts were added to soup, incorporated into black pudding and cooked with cabbage. They were made into purée or sweet chestnut cream and even into bread. Nowadays, many families own a pig, a few lambs, geese and ducks, and perhaps even a few *vaches limousines*, the pale caramel Limousin cattle famous for their delicious meat.

The local cuisine remains uncomplicated and rustic. The former staples—chestnuts, potatoes and cabbage—are still much prized. Cattle

and calves are usually reared to be sold, but the pig feeds the family. In accordance with ancient custom, the slaughter of the pig, *tuer le cochon*, is marked by a three-day celebration with family and friends. The excellent sausages and ham of the region are produced by small family businesses.

The culinary symbol of Limousin is *clafoutis*—batter pudding—an unpretentious but appetizing dish typical of the food of the region. It tastes best when made with alcohol-flavoured batter and small, sweet, black cherries, and should be eaten while still warm. Golden Delicious apples are pressed by the local fruit-growers to make cider.

Festivals
Limoges celebrates a butchers' festival in October. Dournazac and other towns hold chestnut festivals in late October and early November.

Limousin is famous for its excellent sausages and ham.

COCKTAIL NIBBLES AND SNACKS

The French have the perfect phrase for cocktail snacks: *amuse-gueule*—that which amuses the palate. The implication is that, with these foods, enjoyment takes precedence over sustenance. These delightful titbits are not there as part of a meal, but simply for pleasure.

In good French restaurants, imaginative nibbles are served as soon as the customers have ordered. At home, a plate of tiny, tasty snacks will keep guests happy while final preparations are made in the kitchen.

Double the quantities of the snacks in this chapter and you can serve them as starters. Triple them, and add a crisp green salad, and you have a delicious, light main course.

Aperitifs are inevitably served with cocktail snacks. Beware serving a drink that is too strongly-flavoured, however, or you will blunt your guests' taste buds before the meal arrives! Offer still or sparkling wine—or if you are sparing no expense, champagne is the most elegant solution.

With *pâté de foie gras*, a sweet or even a fortified wine is excellent. *Kir*, a blend of blackcurrant liqueur and white wine, has long been a traditional Burgandian aperitif. Less well-known, and therefore a novel choice, would be *bourguignon*, cherry liqueur blended with Burgundy wine.

Pruneaux au Beaufort

Simple • Savoy

Prunes wrapped in bacon

Makes 16

1 tbsp black tea
16 prunes with stones (about 150 g)
50 g Beaufort or Gruyère cheese
50 g Bleu de Savoie or Roquefort
cheese
16 rindless rashers streaky bacon
(about 150 g)

Preparation time: 30 minutes
(plus at least 12 hours' soaking
time)

440 kJ/100 calories per prune

1 Put the tea in a teapot or jug, pour ½ litre boiling water over it and leave to brew for about 2 minutes, then strain. Wash the prunes and soak them overnight in the strained tea.

2 Remove the prunes from the tea and pat dry. Cut each prune at its stalk end and carefully remove the stone. Cut both cheeses into eight pieces. Fill half the prunes with Beaufort cheese and the rest with Bleu de Savoie.

3 Preheat the grill or heat the oven to 250°C (450°F or Mark 8). Wrap the

bacon around the prunes and secure the ends with wooden toothpicks. Arrange the prunes on a baking sheet lined with aluminium foil.

4 Cook them under the grill or in the oven for 3 to 5 minutes on each side, according to the size of the prunes. Remove from under the grill or the oven, taking care as they will be very hot. Cool for about 5 minutes and serve as an appetizer.

Wine: Serve with a Seyssel, a lightly sparkling white wine from Savoy.

Croûte au Beaufort

Prepare in advance • Savoy

Cheese toasts

Serves 8

For the béchamel sauce:
¼ litre milk
7 g butter
½ tbsp flour
salt
freshly grated nutmeg
1 to 2 tbsp crème fraîche
50 g finely grated Beaufort or Gruyère cheese
8 long bread rolls
16 thick slices Beaufort or Gruyère cheese (about 450 g)
lettuce leaves or salad

Preparation time: 40 minutes

1,800 kJ/430 calories per portion

1 Heat the milk. In a separate pan, heat the butter until frothy, stir in the flour and cook over low heat until the flour is lightly browned. Gradually stir in the hot milk. Simmer, covered, over low heat for about 20 minutes. Season to taste with salt and nutmeg.

2 Add the crème fraîche to the cooked sauce. Add the grated cheese and stir until completely melted. Season again.

3 Preheat the grill or heat the oven to 250°C (450°F or Mark 8). Slice the bread rolls in half lengthwise and then hollow them out slightly. Lay a slice of cheese in each hollow.

4 Spoon 1 tbsp béchamel sauce on to the cheese in each halved bread roll, and cook under the grill or on the top shelf of the oven for about 3 minutes, until the cheese filling is golden.

5 Serve the toasts warm, garnished with lettuce leaves, as a cocktail snack, or as a light snack with a salad.

Wine: If you are making the cheese toasts as an appetizer, serve them with Crépy, a light white wine made from the Chasselas grape.

Variation: Use a white baguette, cut into slices, instead of the bread rolls.

Tarte aux champignons

Takes time • Auvergne **Cheese and mushroom flan** *Serves 8 to 10*

For the pastry:
250 g plain flour • 125 g butter
2 tbsp cream or water
salt • butter for greasing

For the topping:
500 g small button mushrooms
30 g butter
salt • freshly ground black pepper
125 g Bleu d'Auvergne or Roquefort
cheese
100 g Cantal or Gruyère cheese
3 eggs • 150 g crème fraîche

Preparation time: 1 hour
(plus 45 minutes' baking time)

1,800 kJ/430 calories per portion
(if serving 10)

1 To make the pastry, knead the flour, butter, cream (or water) and salt to a smooth dough. On a floured work surface, roll out the dough to a thickness of 5 mm. Grease a 26 cm round springform tin (alternatively, use 4 or 5 small tins). Lay the pastry in the tin, lifting the edges slightly. Prick the pastry with a fork. Leave to rest in the refrigerator for about 30 minutes.

2 Meanwhile, make the topping. Trim and wipe the mushrooms. Slice them, using an egg slicer or a knife. Preheat the oven to 200°C (400°F or Mark 6).

3 Melt the butter in a large frying pan over medium heat and sauté the sliced mushrooms, uncovered, in the butter for 3 to 4 minutes, shaking the pan. Season with salt and pepper, and leave to cool slightly. Meanwhile, blind-bake the pastry base in the centre of the oven for 5 to 10 minutes.

4 Crumble the Bleu d'Auvergne into a bowl. Coarsely grate the Cantal cheese and add to the bowl. Mix the eggs and the crème fraîche, season with pepper and stir into the cheese. Scatter the mushrooms in the pastry base, then pour the cheese mixture over them. Bake in the centre of the oven for 45 minutes, until golden-brown. Remove from the tin, cut into 8 to 10 slices and serve warm.

Bleu d'Auvergne

Bleu d'Auvergne, with its engagingly sharp taste, is one of the best known of the French blue cheeses. It could be called a "cow's milk Roquefort" as the same type of penicillium spores are used to "blue" both cheeses.

A good Bleu d'Auvergne is pale and creamy and easily recognizable by the evenly distributed blue veins reaching almost to the rind. The texture of the cheese should be neither granular nor hard, and should have a slightly nutty, piquant flavour with no trace of saltiness. The rind should be firm and dry without being hard.

Bleu d'Auvergne is produced in several regions of France from raw or pasteurized cows' milk. First, the curds are shaped, salted and dried, then penicillium spores from mouldy rye bread are sprinkled into the cheese.

These spread throughout the cheese, producing distinctive bluey-green marbling. It is then left to mature for three months in cool, damp cellars. Finally, it is wrapped in foil to protect its rind during transportation.

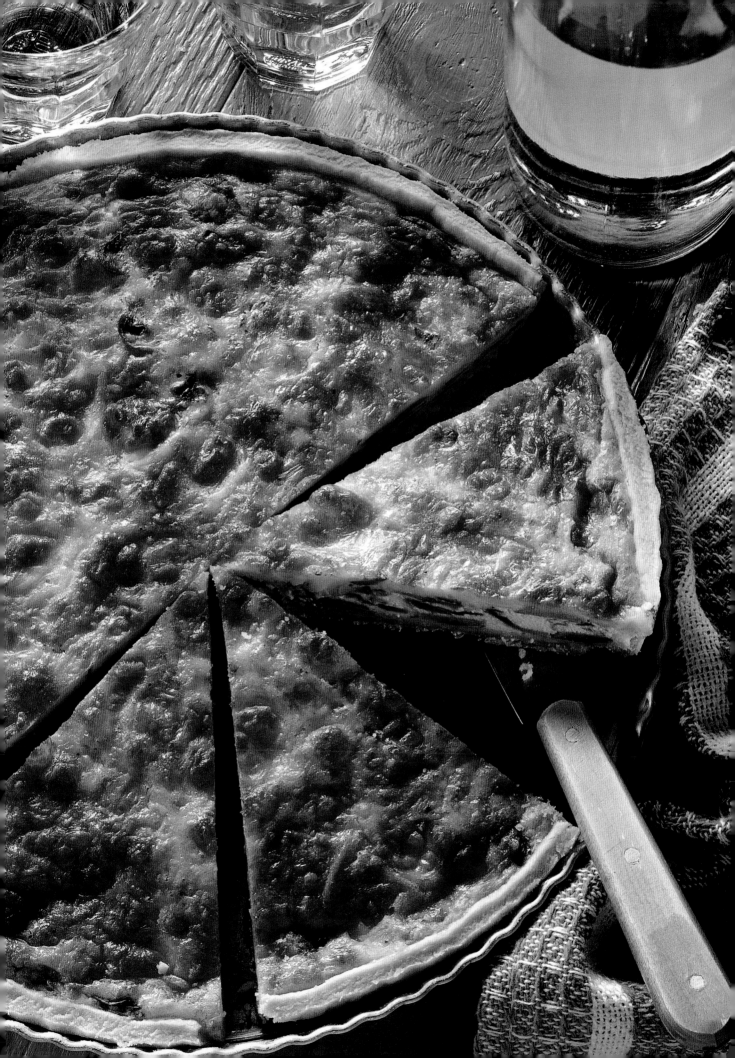

Flammekueche

Alsatian pizza

For the base:
40 g fresh yeast
about 500 g plain flour
1 tsp salt
sugar

For the topping:
4 large onions
30 to 45 g butter
300 to 400 g rindless streaky bacon
2 to 3 tbsp crème fraîche

Preparation time: 1 hour
(plus 2 hours' rising time)

2,000 kJ/480 calories per portion
(if serving 10)

1 To make the base, crumble the yeast into a large bowl, add 250 to 300 g of the flour, the salt, a little sugar and ¼ litre lukewarm water, and mix to a runny dough. Sprinkle with a little more of the flour. Cover the bowl with a tea cloth and leave to rise in a warm place for about 30 minutes.

2 Stir the remaining flour into the dough and knead with floured hands for about 10 minutes, until it no longer sticks to the sides of the bowl. Cover again and leave the dough to rise at room temperature for 1½ hours, until doubled in size. Preheat the oven to 250°C (450°F or Mark 8). Grease two baking sheets. Halve the dough, knead lightly, then roll out and place on the two baking sheets. Blind-bake on the bottom shelf of the oven for 5 minutes.

3 To make the pizza topping, peel the onions and cut into thin rings. Heat the butter in a frying pan. Fry the onions over low heat for 5 to 10 minutes, until translucent. Remove from the heat. Cut the bacon into narrow strips. Spread the base with the crème fraîche and sprinkle with bacon and onion rings.

4 Bake the pizzas one at a time on the bottom shelf of the oven for 10 to 15 minutes, until crisp. Preheat the grill and brown the pizza under the grill for a few minutes before serving. Remove from the heat as soon as the onion rings turn dark brown. Cut the pizza into portions and serve immediately .

Wine: A light white wine, such as Sylvaner, Riesling or Pinot Blanc, goes well with this dish.

Quiche Lorraine

Bacon and egg quiche

For the pastry:
250 g plain flour
125 g butter • 2 tbsp cream
salt

For the topping:
200 g rindless, lean smoked bacon
¼ litre milk • 25 cl double cream
4 eggs
freshly ground black pepper
freshly grated nutmeg

Preparation time: 1 hour
(plus 40 minutes' baking time)

2,300 kJ/550 calories per portion

1 Knead the flour, butter, cream and a little salt to a smooth dough. Line a 28 cm round springform tin with the dough, lifting the edges about 3 cm to form a border. Prick the pastry with a fork. Leave to rest in the refrigerator for at least 30 minutes. After about 15 minutes, preheat the oven to 180°C (350°F or Mark 4).

2 Blind-bake the pastry in the centre of the oven for about 10 to 15 minutes. Meanwhile, cut the bacon into thin strips. Cook in boiling water for about 2 minutes, then drain it thoroughly. Remove the pastry shell from the oven.

3 Pour the milk and cream into a saucepan and warm through over low heat. Remove the pan from the heat. Whisk the eggs into the milk and cream. Season with salt, pepper and nutmeg. Sprinkle the bacon over the pastry shell and pour the egg mixture on top. Bake in the centre of the oven for 30 to 40 minutes, until the topping is golden-brown and set. Turn off the heat and leave the quiche in the oven for about 10 minutes before serving.

Wine: A light white wine from the Côtes de Toul region of Lorraine is extremely good with this bacon quiche.

Gâteau de foies de volaille

Quick • Lyonnais   **Chicken liver pâté**   *Serves 6 to 8*

For the béchamel sauce:
¼ litre milk • 7 g butter
½ tbsp flour
salt • freshly grated nutmeg
1 to 2 tbsp crème fraîche

For the liver pâté:
2 slices pain de mie or sliced white bread
about 5 cl milk • 4 garlic cloves
500 g chicken livers
2 eggs
7 g fresh parsley
salt • freshly ground black pepper
butter for greasing

Preparation time: 40 minutes
(plus 30 to 35 minutes' baking time and 12 hours' standing time)

790 kJ/190 calories per portion (if serving 8)

1 To make the sauce, heat the milk in a pan. In a separate pan, heat the butter until frothy, stir in the flour and cook over low heat until the flour is lightly browned. Gradually stir in the hot milk. Simmer, covered, over low heat for 20 minutes. Season with salt and nutmeg. Stir in the crème fraîche.

2 Meanwhile, soak the bread in the 5 cl milk. Peel the garlic. Purée the garlic and chicken livers in a food processor. Separate the eggs. Wash, dry and chop the parsley. Squeeze the bread dry and stir into the livers with the egg yolks and parsley. Remove the sauce from the heat. Carefully stir the liver mixture into the sauce and leave to cool. Season with salt and pepper.

3 Preheat the oven to 150°C (300°F or Mark 2). Whisk the egg whites with a little salt until stiff, then fold into the cooled liver mixture. Grease a 1 litre ovenproof terrine. Transfer the pâté to the terrine and bake in the centre of the oven for 30 to 35 minutes, until lightly browned. Leave to cool, then chill in the refrigerator for about 12 hours before serving. Remove from the refrigerator 30 minutes before serving to bring to room temperature.

4 Spread the pâté thickly on slices of baguette. Serve with olives, pickled gherkins or crunchy radishes, if liked.

Wine: As this is a full-flavoured pâté, serve it with a soft, fruity wine, such as Beaujolais Nouveau or a Gamay.

Cou de l'oie farci aux truffes

Prepare in advance • Alsace

Truffle-stuffed goose neck

Serves 6 to 8

1 slice pain de mie or sliced white bread
5 cl milk
1 shallot • ½ cooking apple
60 g goose fat
1 small truffle • 1 goose liver
125 g pork sausage meat
1 small egg
salt • freshly ground black pepper
freshly grated nutmeg
brandy
skin of 1 goose neck (ordered in advance from the butcher) or 30 to 40 cm sausage skin

Preparation time: 1 hour (plus 24 hours' standing time)

1,100 kJ/260 calories per portion (if serving 8)

1 Soak the bread in the milk. Peel and finely chop the shallot and apple. Heat 30 g of the goose fat in a frying pan and fry the chopped shallot and apple, uncovered, over medium heat for about 5 minutes, until golden-brown, then leave to cool. Scrub, wash and finely chop the truffle.

2 Remove the sinews from the goose liver. Cut the liver into small pieces. Squeeze the bread dry, then mix with the sausage meat, egg, shallot, apple and truffle. Season generously with salt, pepper and grated nutmeg. Stir thoroughly, then add a dash of brandy.

3 Preheat the oven to 180°C (350°F or Mark 4). Place the remaining goose fat in a roasting pan and melt it on the

bottom shelf of the oven. Sew up the narrow end of the goose neck with kitchen twine. Starting at the opposite end, fill the neck loosely with stuffing, then sew up the opening. Place the stuffed goose neck in the hot fat in the roasting pan and cook in the oven for 20 minutes, turning from time to time.

4 Remove the goose neck from the pan and leave until quite cold. Chill in the refrigerator for at least 24 hours, then slice and serve it alone, or on small pieces of toast with lettuce leaves.

Wine: If you prefer white wine, serve a Pinot Blanc. A velvety Alsatian Pinot Noir is a good choice if you prefer red.

HORS-D'ŒUVRE

No French meal is complete without an hors-d'œuvre. It ushers in the main meal with a flourish, and stimulates the palate for the courses that are to come. And because it is the first food on the table, it is eaten with an attention and relish that is rewarding for cook and diner alike.

The hors-d'œuvre may consist of salad, smoked fish or pâté, or any kind of soup—bouillon, consommé or cream. When the weather is cold, French family meals often include a thick soup or broth, accompanied by vin de pays.

Eastern France and the Massif Central boast a great variety of rustic but refined starters. Many are based on cheese, which is widely produced in these two regions, while a simple but substantial starter would be a selection of local sausages or a home-made terrine. *Escargots aux beurre d'ail* from Burgundy has become a classic of French cuisine.

With hearty, meat-based hors-d'œuvre, serve a light red wine from the same region as the dish. A crisp white wine is a better choice with starters of fish or poultry. A vinaigrette or lemon juice dressing on a salad tends to spoil the flavour of wine; it is better here simply to provide a carafe of water on the table.

Salade à la Bressane

Bresse-style chicken salad

Simple • Bresse

Serves 4 to 6

150 g fresh or 15 to 30 g dried morels
¼ litre chicken stock (see Note)
12.5 cl dry white wine (for example, Seyssel)
about 800 g chicken breasts
2 or 3 eggs
about 24 thin spears green asparagus (about 500 g)
1 lettuce
1 bunch small radishes
3 sprigs each fresh parsley, chives and chervil

For the vinaigrette:
3 tbsp sherry vinegar
salt
freshly ground black pepper
3 tbsp groundnut oil
6 tbsp hazelnut oil

Preparation time: 35 minutes (plus 1 to 2 hours´ soaking time and 1½ hours for making the stock, if necessary)

1,600 kJ/380 calories per portion (if serving 6)

1 If using dried morels, soak them in ¼ litre warm water for 1 to 2 hours. Remove them from the water and strain the water through a coffee filter bag. If using fresh morels, rinse them thoroughly under cold running water. Cook the morels, uncovered, over high heat with the soaking water, or ¼ litre water with a little salt, for 10 minutes, or until the liquid has evaporated.

2 Bring the chicken stock and wine to the boil in a saucepan. Add the chicken breasts, cover and simmer over low heat for 20 to 25 minutes, until the meat is cooked. Remove from the pan.

3 Meanwhile, put the eggs in a pan of cold water. Bring to the boil and cook over medium heat for 6 to 8 minutes. Rinse in cold water, shell and halve.

4 Wash and peel the asparagus. Trim the tips to a length of 6 to 8 cm. (Save the rest of the asparagus to use for another recipe.) Cook the tips in a pan of salted water over medium heat for 7 to 10 minutes, until tender. Prepare a bowl of cold water with ice cubes in it. As soon as the asparagus is cooked, rinse it in the iced water *(above)*.

5 Divide the lettuce into single leaves, wash and dry in a salad spinner. Cut off the radish leaves, then wash and dry

the radishes. Wash the herbs, shake, then pat dry and chop finely.

6 Mix the vinegar, salt and pepper in a small bowl. Stir in the groundnut and hazelnut oils a little at a time.

7 Bone the cooked chicken breasts and cut the meat across the grain into equal-sized slices *(above)*.

8 Divide the lettuce leaves between individual salad bowls or plates and arrange the sliced chicken, morels, asparagus, radishes and halved eggs on top. Sprinkle with the herbs. Pour a little of the dressing over the salad and serve immediately, accompanied by the rest of the dressing and crusty white baguettes.

Note: It is very easy to make your own stock. For 1 litre, wash 500 g giblets (chicken, turkey or goose, according to the recipe). Trim and wash ½ leek, 1 carrot and 1 stick celery, and bind them together with kitchen twine. Peel 1 medium-sized onion and spike with 5 cloves. Place the giblets and the vegetables in a deep saucepan, cover with 1.5 litres water and bring to the boil over high heat, then add a little salt. Cover and cook over medium heat for about 1 hour. Strain the stock and skim off the fat when cool.

Salade des vignerons

Wine-growers' salad

Easy · Champagne

Serves 4

200 g mixed salad (lamb's lettuce, nasturtium and dandelion leaves)
few chives
5 sprigs each fresh parsley, chervil and tarragon
salt · freshly ground black pepper
12.5 cl verjuice (see Note) or 10cl unsweetened grape juice mixed with the juice of 1 lemon
100 g rindless streaky bacon
1 garlic clove
1 thick slice cooked ham (200 g)

Preparation time: 20 minutes

1,600 kJ/380 calories per portion

1 Trim and wash the salad leaves and dry them in a salad spinner. Wash the chives, parsley, chervil and tarragon, shake dry and chop finely.

2 Place the salad in a large serving bowl. Sprinkle with salt and pepper, and drizzle with verjuice, or mixture of grape juice and lemon juice.

3 Cut the bacon into small strips and fry in a frying pan over medium heat for 2 to 3 minutes, until golden-brown. Peel the garlic and cut in half. Rub the ham with the cut surfaces of the garlic, then cut the ham into thin slivers.

4 Sprinkle the ham, bacon and hot fat in the frying pan over the salad. Mix thoroughly. Sprinkle with the chopped herbs and serve immediately.

Note: Verjuice, *Verjus* or *jus de raisin vert* is the juice of unripe grapes. It gives a sour, piquant flavour to food. Dishes made from poultry stewed in verjuice are very popular in France. In England, verjuice used to be made from sour green apples, and used as a condiment instead of vinegar. It is seldom used nowadays.

Salade à la Lyonnaise

Herring salad from Lyon

Simple · Lyonnais

Serves 4

8 herring fillets, canned in oil
4 tbsp red wine vinegar
1 heaped tsp hot mustard
salt
freshly ground black pepper
sugar
12 tbsp virgin olive oil
200 g mixed salad leaves
3 to 4 sprigs fresh parsley
2 tbsp vinegar
4 eggs
4 small slices coarse rye bread
2 garlic cloves

Preparation time: 50 minutes

2,900 kJ/690 calories per portion

1 Soak the herring fillets in water for about 30 minutes. Mix the vinegar, mustard, salt, pepper and sugar. Stir in the oil. (The dressing should have a strong mustard flavour.)

2 Trim and wash the salad leaves and dry thoroughly in a salad spinner. Tear into small pieces and place in a salad bowl. Wash the parsley, shake, pat dry and chop finely.

3 Bring 1 litre water to the boil in a saucepan with 2 tbsp vinegar. Break the eggs into a ladle, one at a time, and slide them into the water. Poach over low heat for 3 to 4 minutes.

4 Pat the herring fillets dry and cut into strips about 1 cm wide. Toast the bread on both sides. Peel and halve the garlic. Rub the hot toast with the cut surfaces of the garlic, then cut the toast into small dice.

5 Toss the salad thoroughly in the dressing. Carefully fold in the herring strips and garlic croûtons. Divide the salad between four individual plates, and place a warm poached egg on top of each one. Sprinkle with the chopped parsley and serve immediately.

Note: Make sure you use only very fresh eggs from a reliable source. The very young, the elderly, pregnant women and anyone with problems with their immune system are advised not to eat raw or very lightly cooked eggs because of the risk of salmonella.

Escargots aux beurre d'ail

Snails with garlic butter

Prepare in advance • Burgundy

Serves 4

250 g canned Burgundy snails
4 tbsp marc de Bourgogne (brandy)
48 snail shells

For the garlic butter:
10 garlic cloves
15 g fresh parsley
1 tsp salt
freshly ground pepper
500 g slightly softened butter
about 2 kg coarse salt (optional)

Preparation time: 50 minutes

4,300 kJ/1,000 calories per portion

1 Place the snails, with their juice, and the marc de Bourgogne in a saucepan. Bring to the boil and cook, uncovered, over high heat for 1 to 2 minutes. Remove the snails and drain thoroughly on paper towels.

2 To make the garlic butter, peel the garlic. Wash the parsley and shake dry. Finely chop the garlic and parsley. Blend the chopped garlic and parsley, salt and pepper into the butter with a fork. Check the seasoning.

3 Spoon a little garlic butter into each shell with a teaspoon. Place a snail in each shell and then seal the shells with the rest of the butter.

4 Arrange the snails on four snail plates (snail plates are specially designed with hollows which prevent the butter running away as it melts). If you do not have any snail plates, cook the snails in a single layer on a thick bed of coarse salt in four ovenproof dishes.

5 Preheat the oven to 225°C (425°F or Mark 7). Heat the snails in the centre of the oven for about 7 minutes, until the butter begins to bubble. Remove from the oven and serve immediately with warm baguettes.

Wine: White Burgundy is the best wine to serve with this dish.

Jambon persillé

Ham in parsley aspic

More complex • Burgundy

Serves 10

2.5 kg leg of raw ham
1 litre white wine
1 onion • 5 cloves
5 garlic cloves • 1 carrot
3 to 4 pig's trotters
1 bouquet garni
10 black peppercorns

For the parsley layer:
60 g fresh parsley
12. 5 cl wine vinegar
3 garlic cloves

Preparation time: 1 hour
(plus 2 days' soaking time, 2 hours'
cooking time and 12 hours'
chilling time)

3,600 kJ/860 calories per portion

1 Soak the ham in water for 24 to 48 hours to remove the salt, changing the water frequently. Bring the wine to the boil with 1 to 2 litres water. Peel the onion and spike with the cloves. Peel the garlic. Wash the carrot. Place the ham, carrot, pig's trotters, bouquet garni, onion, garlic and peppercorns in the pan with the wine and water. Cover and simmer over very low heat for about 2 hours. Check that the ham is thoroughly cooked before removing from the stock. Detach the meat from the bones and cut into chunks. Strain and skim the stock.

2 Wash the parsley and shake dry. Reserve a few sprigs and finely chop the rest of the leaves. Marinate the chopped parsley in the vinegar for 10 minutes. Peel the garlic and chop finely. Line a 2 litre terrine with half the chopped parsley and sprinkle with a little garlic. Press the ham into the terrine a little at a time, spreading thinly with the rest of the marinated parsley and sprinkling with garlic, until all the ingredients are used up. Pour 12.5 cl of the warm stock into the terrine. Cover with foil, with a weight on top. Leave to set in the refrigerator. Cut into thick slices, garnish with the parsley sprigs and serve with bread.

Note: If a very firm aspic is preferred, soak 1 or 2 leaves of gelatine, dissolve them in ¼ litre of the stock and pour this over the ham while still warm.

Quenelles de brochet

More complicated • Lyonnais   **Pike dumplings**   *Serves 4*

¼ litre milk
100 g butter, plus extra for greasing
salt • 200 g plain flour
4 egg yolks
freshly ground white pepper
freshly grated nutmeg
500 g pike or whiting, cleaned
3 or 4 egg whites
fresh chervil leaves to garnish

For the mushroom sauce:
½ litre milk
30 g butter • 1 tbsp flour
200 g crème fraîche
1 shallot • juice of 1 lemon
500 g button mushrooms

Preparation time: 1¾ hours
(plus at least 2 hours' chilling time)

3,200 kJ/760 calories per portion

1 To make the choux pastry, bring the milk, the 100 g butter and salt to the boil in a saucepan. Add the flour all at once, then stir for 5 minutes with a wooden spoon until the dough comes away from the sides of the saucepan. Remove from the heat and leave to cool slightly. Stir the egg yolks, one at a time, into the dough. Season with pepper and nutmeg. Cool completely. Skin and bone the fish, then purée in a food processor with the egg whites. Blend the purée into the dough, season and then chill for 2 hours.

2 In a wide saucepan, bring 2 litres salted water to the boil. Shape the dough into oval quenelles, using two tablespoons. Cook three at a time in the water over very low heat for about 5 minutes. Drain on paper towels.

3 To make the sauce, heat the milk in a pan. In another pan, heat half the butter until frothy. Stir the flour into the butter and cook until the roux is lightly browned, stirring constantly. Gradually stir in the milk. Cover and simmer over low heat for 20 minutes, then stir in the crème fraîche.

4 Preheat the oven to 175°C (350°F or Mark 4). Peel and finely chop the shallot, then place it in a pan with the remaining butter, lemon juice, salt and 2 litres water. Wipe the mushrooms, slice, then simmer, uncovered, in the water, over low heat for 5 minutes. Drain, and add to the sauce. Bring to the boil and season with white pepper. Wash the chervil and shake dry.

5 Butter a gratin dish. Arrange the quenelles in the dish and pour over the sauce. Bake in the centre of the oven for 10 minutes, until the quenelles rise. Serve sprinkled with the chervil.

Gâteau de foies blonds

Simple · Bresse

Warm chicken liver pâté

Serves 2

150 g chicken livers
1 tbsp flour
1 egg · 1 egg yolk
1 tsp crème fraîche
12.5 cl milk
salt · freshly ground white pepper
freshly grated nutmeg
7 g fresh parsley
1 garlic clove
butter for greasing

For the crayfish sauce:
60 g butter
500 g crayfish (ask the fishmonger
to plunge them briefly in boiling
water)
2 cl brandy
12.5 cl dry white wine
10 cl double cream
powdered saffron

Preparation time: 1 hour

4,000 kJ/950 calories per portion

1 Preheat the oven to 150°C (300°F or Mark 2). Wash the chicken livers, pat dry, and chop finely in a blender. One after the other, add the flour, egg, egg yolk, crème fraîche and milk. Rub the mixture through a sieve and season generously with salt, pepper and nutmeg. Wash the parsley and pat dry. Peel the garlic. Finely chop the parsley and garlic together and add to the liver mixture. Butter a ½ litre terrine. Turn the pâté into the greased terrine and cover with a lid or foil with a hole in it. Stand the terrine in a roasting pan half-filled with water and bake in the centre of the oven for 30 minutes until the pâté is set.

2 Using two large frying pans, heat 30 g butter in each and fry the crayfish until bright pink on both sides. Pour the brandy into a ladle, warm it over the pan, then pour it over the crayfish. Carefully ignite the brandy and flambé the crayfish. Remove from the pan.

3 Add the wine to the pan and reduce over medium heat to about 2 tbsp. Add the double cream. Season with salt, pepper and a little saffron. Return the crayfish to the sauce and cook over very low heat for 8 to 10 minutes.

4 When the pâté is cooked, turn off the heat and leave it to stand in the cooling oven for about 10 minutes, then turn out on to a warmed serving dish. Pour the sauce over the pâté and garnish with the crayfish.

Note: In Bresse, this recipe is made with chicken livers from the celebrated chickens of that region. The pâté is so delicious it is worth trebling the quantities shown and cooking it in six small gratin dishes, 8 cm in diameter. The pâté is also excellent served with the crayfish sauce recipe on page 97.

Quenelles de volaille

Chicken dumplings with creamed lentils

Takes time • Auvergne

Serves 4

1 litre chicken stock (see Note, page 38)
2 chicken breasts (about 200 g each)
1 egg white
150 g crème fraîche
salt • freshly ground black pepper
200 g Puy lentils
1 onion • 3 cloves • 1 carrot
1 bouquet garni
mineral water
butter for greasing
fresh chervil leaves

Preparation time: 1¾ hours (plus 1½ hours for making the stock, if necessary)

1,700 kJ/400 calories per portion

1 Heat the stock in a saucepan. Wash the chicken breasts and add to the pan. Cover and simmer for 15 minutes. Remove the chicken from the pan and leave to cool. Reserve the stock. When the meat is cold, purée it in a blender or food processor with the egg white and 50 g crème fraîche. Season with salt and pepper, then chill for 1 hour.

2 Meanwhile, wash the lentils. Peel the onion and spike it with the cloves. Wash and peel the carrot. Place the lentils, onion and carrot in a saucepan with the bouquet garni, cover with mineral water, and season. Cover and simmer over low heat for 45 minutes, adding more water, if necessary.

3 Preheat the oven to 180°C (350°F or Mark 4). Butter a gratin dish. Shape the chicken mixture into 12 quenelles, using two tablespoons. Arrange them in the dish and bake in the centre of the oven for about 15 minutes. Wash the chervil and pat dry.

4 Remove the bouquet garni, onion and carrot from the lentils. Purée the lentils with 2 to 3 tbsp stock and rub through a coarse sieve. Add the rest of the crème fraîche, then bring to the boil to make a thick sauce. Season with salt and pepper. Divide the sauce between four individual plates. Place three quenelles on top of each one and serve at once, garnished with chervil.

Puy lentils

The centre of France is great lentil country, and those of Le Puy in the Auvergne are widely considered the finest. Puy lentils are renowned for their colour, a deep green marbled with turquoise—a result of the volcanic soil that nourishes them. Their full, peppery flavour makes them the ideal accompaniment for robust meats such as pork, venison and game. They are also used to thicken soups, and make delicious puréed sauces.

Every October, market stands in southern and central France proudly advertise their stocks of *"lentilles vert du Puy, nouvelle recolte"*. Puy lentils are the only variety to merit the AOC (Appellation d'Origine Contrôlée) quality label.

Like all green and brown lentils, Puy lentils keep their shape when cooked. They do not need soaking, just a brief wash before being simmered in stock or water until they are just tender (in France, mineral water is often used to obtain a better flavour).

Lentils are full of protein as well as generous amounts of vitamins and minerals. Once dried, they will keep for up to six months if stored in a dark place.

Potage aux châtaignes

Chestnut soup

Takes time • Limousin

Serves 6

1 kg chestnuts • 1 stick celery
1 litre mineral water or beef stock
(see Note, page 53)
300 g onions
1 leek • 2 carrots
4 small white turnips
2 floury potatoes
about ¼ litre milk
2 tbsp crème fraîche
salt • freshly ground black pepper
6 small slices coarse rye bread

Preparation time: 1¾ hours
(plus 1½ hours for making the
stock, if necessary)

2,300 kJ/550 calories per portion

1 Preheat the oven to 180°C (350°F or Mark 4). Score each of the chestnuts across the top with a sharp knife, then arrange them in a baking tray and pour 12.5 cl water over them. Roast in the centre of the oven for 7 to 8 minutes, then peel away the outer shells and inner skins with the point of a knife. Cut the chestnuts in half and discard any damaged ones.

2 Wash the celery and cut into large chunks. Place the chestnut halves and celery chunks in a large saucepan with enough mineral water or stock to cover them. Cover the pan and cook over medium heat for about 20 minutes.

3 Meanwhile, peel the onions. Trim and wash the leek. Wash and peel the carrots, turnips and potatoes. Roughly chop all the vegetables and add them to the chestnuts and celery. Re-cover and cook for another 20 minutes, until the chestnuts are tender.

4 Purée the soup in a blender or food processor. Add the milk and crème fraîche, and season to taste with salt and pepper. Return briefly to the boil over medium heat. While the soup is reheating, toast the bread and cut it into small dice. Pour the soup into a tureen and sprinkle the croûtons on top. Serve at once.

Soupe dauphinoise

Cream of sorrel soup

Takes time • Dauphiné

Serves 4

100 g dried white haricot beans
4 medium-sized onions • 3 cloves
3 leeks
1 stick celery
4 carrots
500 g pie or stewing veal
1 litre mineral water
75 g butter
400 g tomatoes
salt
freshly ground white pepper
100 to 150 g sorrel
250 g crème fraîche, at room
temperature

Preparation time: 1½ hours
(plus 12 hours' soaking time
and 1 hour's cooking time)

3,000 kJ/710 calories per portion

1 Place the beans in a bowl and cover with water. Leave to soak overnight.

2 Peel one onion and spike it with the cloves. Trim and wash one leek and the celery. Wash and peel one carrot. Put these vegetables in a saucepan with the veal and the mineral water. Bring to the boil, then cover and simmer over low heat for about 1 hour.

3 Meanwhile, peel or trim the remaining onions, carrots and leeks, before washing and chopping them. Heat 50 g of the butter in a large pan and sauté the vegetables over low heat for about 20 minutes, stirring occasionally. Peel and quarter the tomatoes and remove the seeds. Drain the beans and put them in a pan

with enough water to cover. Bring to the boil for 10 minutes, then drain and add the beans to the sautéed vegetables with the tomatoes. Season the veal stock with salt and pepper. Strain it, saving the onion (you can use the meat in another dish). Add the stock and the onion to the vegetables and beans. Cover the pan and simmer over low heat for 1 hour.

4 Discard the whole onion. Purée the soup in a food processor or blender, and season with salt and pepper. Wash the sorrel, shake dry and shred. Melt the rest of the butter and fry the sorrel for a few seconds. Divide the sorrel and the crème fraîche between four warmed soup bowls. Pour the hot soup into the bowls and serve immediately.

Soupe au Cantal

Not difficult • Auvergne · **Onion soup with cheese** · *Serves 4 to 6*

4 medium-sized onions
2 to 4 garlic cloves
30 g butter
1.5 litres beef stock (see Note, page 53)
freshly ground black pepper
4 to 6 slices brown bread
400 g sliced Cantal or Gruyère cheese
10 cl double cream, at room temperature

Preparation time: 45 minutes (plus 1½ hours for making the stock, if necessary)

1,800 kJ/430 calories per portion (if serving 6)

1 Peel and thinly slice the onions and garlic. Heat the butter in a large pan and fry the sliced onions and garlic, uncovered, over medium heat for about 5 minutes, until golden-brown. Add the stock, cover and simmer over low heat for 15 to 20 minutes. Season to taste with pepper.

2 While the onion soup is cooking, preheat the oven to 150°C (300°F or Mark 2) for 10 to 15 minutes, then turn it off. Toast the bread, then cut the slices in half. Arrange the toast and cheese in alternate layers in an ovenproof soup tureen. Add the onion soup and warm it through in the oven for 10 minutes. Just before serving, swirl the double cream on top.

Note: Instead of using a large tureen, you can cook and serve the soup in four to six individual bowls.

Variation: Gratinée Lyonnaise
(Onion soup with port)
Using 800 g onions, 50 g butter and 1½ litres stock, prepare the onion soup as described in the recipe. Mix 1 fresh egg with 3 to 4 tbsp port, then stir the mixture into the soup. Do not allow the soup to return to the boil. Arrange 4 to 6 slices of baguette in an ovenproof tureen. Pour the soup on top and sprinkle with 225 g grated Gruyère cheese. Bake in the centre of the oven at 250°C (450°F or Mark 8) for about 5 minutes, until the cheese is melted and golden.

Soupe au Beaufort

Easy • Savoy **Vegetable soup with cheese toasts** *Serves 6 to 8*

3 sticks celery
3 medium-sized leeks
3 small white turnips
75 g butter
750 g waxy potatoes
1.5 litres mineral water
salt
freshly ground black pepper
¼ litre milk, or 12.5 cl milk and
125 g crème fraîche
½ large baguette
200 g sliced Beaufort or Gruyère
cheese
fresh chervil leaves for garnish

Preparation time: 50 minutes

1,200 kJ/290 calories per portion
(if serving 8)

1 Remove the leaves from the celery and the green parts from the leeks. Wash both vegetables, then cut into 5 mm slices. Peel the turnips and dice or cut into 1 cm strips. Heat the butter in a large pan and sauté the vegetables over low heat for 3 to 5 minutes.

2 Peel, wash, quarter and thinly slice the potatoes, and add to the rest of the vegetables with the mineral water. Season with salt and pepper. Bring to the boil over high heat, then cover and simmer over low heat for 10 minutes, stirring from time to time.

3 Add the milk, then re-cover the pan and simmer the soup for a further 10 minutes, until the potatoes are tender. Season to taste with salt.

4 Preheat the grill or heat the oven to 250°C (450°F or Mark 8). Slice the baguette and lay the sliced cheese on top. Cook under the grill or at the top of the oven until the cheese melts. Wash the chervil and pat dry.

5 Pour the soup into a warmed tureen or individual soup bowls. Arrange the toasted cheese slices on top. Garnish with chervil leaves and serve at once.

Wine: Crépy, a pleasantly dry white wine from Savoy, is good with this soup, and with Beaufort cheese.

Soupe de potiron en croûte

Pumpkin soup with a puff pastry crust

Prepare in advance • Savoy   *Serves 6*

For the puff pastry:
125 g plain flour
¼ tsp salt
150 to 200 g very fresh butter,
straight from the refrigerator (the
more you use, the better it tastes)
3 tbsp ice-cold water
1 egg yolk for glazing

For the pumpkin soup:
100 g onions or shallots
1 fennel bulb (about 200 g)
25 g butter
1 kg pumpkin
1 litre beef stock (see Note)
150 g crème fraîche
salt
freshly ground black pepper
100 g coarsely grated Beaufort or
Gruyère cheese

Preparation time: 1¼ hours
(plus 2 hours' resting time and
1½ hours for making the stock, if
necessary)

3,200 kJ/760 calories per portion

1 To make the puff pastry, mix the flour and salt together. Cut 75 g of the butter into small pieces and rub in.

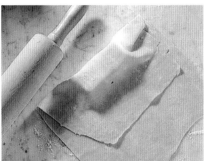

2 Stir in the water and knead to a soft dough. Leave to rest in the refrigerator for 30 minutes then, on a floured work surface, roll out the dough to a long rectangle. Shape the rest of the butter into a slab about 2 cm thick and place in the middle of the dough. Fold both ends of the rectangle over the butter *(above)*. Roll out the dough, sprinkle with flour, then wrap in a cloth and chill for a further 30 minutes. Roll it out three more times at 30 minute intervals. Each time, fold both ends of the rectangle over the middle section, roll out, wrap and chill again. Finally, roll the dough into a square.

3 Meanwhile, peel and roughly chop the onions. Trim and wash the fennel, removing the feathery leaves. Chop it into small dice. Melt the butter in a large saucepan and fry the onions until transparent, then add the fennel. Peel the pumpkin, discarding seeds and fibres. Cut the flesh into chunks and add to the vegetables in the pan. Fry over low heat until lightly browned, stirring constantly. Add the stock, cover and cook over medium heat for 20 minutes. Preheat the oven to 200°C (400°F or Mark 6).

4 Purée the soup in a blender or food processor. Stir in the crème fraîche and season with salt and pepper. Pour the soup into six ovenproof soup bowls or mugs and sprinkle the cheese on top. Roll out the pastry and cut out six circles, slightly larger than the rims of the bowls. Place a pastry circle on top of each bowl and seal firmly *(above)*. Brush the pastry with egg yolk. Bake in the centre of the oven for 10 minutes. Place the bowls on saucers as they will be very hot, and serve at once.

Note: To make home-made beef stock, wash 500 to 750 g stewing beef. Trim and wash ½ leek, 1 carrot and 1 stick celery, and tie together with kitchen twine. Peel 1 medium-sized onion and spike it with 5 cloves. Place the meat, vegetables and 10 to 15 peppercorns in a pan with 2 litres water. Add salt, then bring briefly to the boil over high heat. Simmer, covered, over medium heat for 1 hour. Strain the stock and skim off the fat. This makes 1.5 litres stock. Save the meat for another dish.

Variation: The soup can be served without the pastry, if preferred. Pour into a tureen, sprinkle with croûtons *(see step 5, page 59)*, and serve grated cheese separately so that everyone can help themselves.

FISH

I n the rushing streams and cold lakes of eastern France and the Massif Central, there is still an abundance of trout, carp, char and tench. Local anglers take full advantage of this rich stock of fish: there is little to beat French freshwater fish caught in season. Trout and carp are farmed, too, to boost supplies and provide produce for the export market.

The French love fish—especially those caught close to home—and prepare wonderful dishes with them. Fish is often cooked in a rich, creamy wine sauce thickened with egg yolks, as in *matelote de truite* (recipe, page 59). To accompany this kind of dish, simply serve the same wine as you have used in the sauce—best of all a wine from the area in which the fish was caught.

Regions can be very possessive about popular dishes. There is a long-running dispute between Burgundy and Franche-Comté as to which region created *pauchouse* (recipe, page 64), a stew made from fish caught in the River Doubs. The argument centres on whether the dish originated in Verdun-sur-le-Doubs, on the borders of Burgundy, or in Franche-Comté, through which most of the Doubs flows.

As the dish is also sometimes known as *pochouse*, there is an additional dispute about the name and where it comes from. A *pochouse* is the bag in which anglers keep their catch—which doesn't help to settle the matter. You can smile over this little altercation as you enjoy the dish!

Poisson à l'ancienne

Easy • Savoy **Char with mushroom sauce** *Serves 4*

*2 cleaned char (about 500 g each),
or 4 cleaned salmon trout (about
300 g each)
juice of 1 lemon
salt
freshly ground black pepper
30 to 45 g butter for greasing*

*For the mushroom sauce:
600 g mixed mushrooms (for
example, ceps, chanterelles and
chestnut mushrooms)
2 to 4 garlic cloves
50 g butter
¼ litre dry white wine (for example,
Crépy)
juice of 1 lemon
100 g crème fraîche
salt
freshly ground black pepper
sugar (optional)
fresh sprigs parsley*

Preparation time: 55 minutes

2,700 kJ/640 calories per portion

1 Wash the fish and pat dry. Sprinkle them inside and out with lemon juice. Leave to stand for about 15 minutes. Season the fish inside and out with salt and pepper. Butter an ovenproof baking dish and place the fish in it.

2 Trim the mushrooms and wipe with paper towel *(above)*, or rinse briefly under cold running water, then pat thoroughly dry. Cut larger mushrooms into 1 cm-thick slices. Preheat the oven to 180°C (350°F or Mark 4).

3 Peel and halve the garlic cloves and cut into thin slivers. Heat the butter in a large frying pan and briefly sauté the garlic. Add the mushrooms and cook over high heat, turning frequently, until all the pan juices have evaporated.

4 Add the white wine to the pan. Mix the lemon juice and crème fraîche, then stir it into the mushroom mixture. Season with salt and pepper and, if liked, a little sugar.

5 Spoon a little of the mushroom sauce into the body cavities of the fish *(above)*. Pour the rest of the sauce over them.

6 Bake the char for about 20 minutes (trout need only about 10 minutes) in the centre of the oven, basting frequently with the sauce. Wash the parsley, shake, then pat dry. Tear off the leaves.

7 At the end of the cooking time, transfer the fish to a serving dish and keep warm, then pour the sauce over them; the sauce can be boiled to reduce it a little, if wished. Alternatively, serve straight from the baking dish, garnished with the parsley sprigs, and accompanied by creamed potatoes *(see page 108)*. Divide the fish into portions at the table.

Wine: The same white wine that is used in the sauce—preferably Crépy, a dry Chasselas from Lake Geneva—is perfect with this dish.

Note: Char *(omble chevalier)* is a rare treat. It is a large, delicately flavoured type of trout, native to the alpine lakes of Savoy, where the water temperature is less than 12°C. The colour of the flesh varies from pale pink to red. It is firm, but very tender.

Matelote de truite

Trout cooked in red wine and cream   *Serves 4*

4 cleaned trout (about 200 to 300 g each)
juice of 1½ lemons
1 small onion
300 g small button mushrooms
about 75 g butter
salt
freshly ground black pepper
1 large shallot
¼ litre fish stock (see Note)
¼ litre fruity red wine (for example, Pinot Noir de Toul)
2 egg yolks
100 g crème fraîche
16 slices from a white French loaf
15 g fresh parsley
1 unwaxed lemon

Preparation time: 1¼ hours
(plus 45 minutes for making the fish stock, if necessary)

3,600 kJ/860 calories per portion

1 Wash the trout and pat dry. Sprinkle them inside and out with the juice of one of the lemons, and leave to stand for about 15 minutes.

2 Peel and finely chop the onion. Clean and slice the mushrooms. Heat 30 g of the butter in a saucepan and fry the onion over low heat for about 5 minutes, until transparent. Add the mushrooms and fry, uncovered, over medium heat for 2 to 3 minutes, then season with salt and pepper. Continue to cook over low heat for 5 minutes, then set aside.

3 Preheat the oven to 180°C (350°F or Mark 4). Grease an ovenproof dish with 15 g of the butter. Peel and finely chop the shallot and sprinkle into the dish. Season the trout inside and out with salt and pepper, then cut each one crosswise into strips 5 to 6 cm wide and arrange on top of the chopped shallot. Pour the hot fish stock and red wine over the fish and bake in the centre of the oven for 10 to 15 minutes. Turn off the heat and keep the trout warm in the cooling oven.

4 Pour the fish stock into a saucepan and boil over high heat until reduced to 3 tbsp. Mix together the egg yolks, crème fraîche and the rest of the lemon juice. Reduce the heat under the stock to low. Add the cream mixture and stir briefly. Add the mushrooms, season with salt and pepper, then pour the mixture over the trout in the oven.

5 Cut the bread slices into small dice and toast them in a large frying pan, without any fat, over high heat until golden-brown. Remove the frying pan from the heat, add 30 g butter to the hot pan, then toss the bread in the melted butter.

6 Wash the parsley, shake dry and finely chop. Wash the lemon and cut lengthwise into eight wedges. Remove the trout from the oven and sprinkle with the parsley and croûtons. Garnish with the lemon wedges and serve.

Wine: Serve with Pinot Noir de Toul, a red wine from Lorraine.

Note: It is easy to make home-made fish stock. For ½ to ¾ litre, peel and dice 1 onion and fry briefly in 30 g butter. Add 5 to 6 trimmed mushrooms and 500 g washed fish trimmings, and fry for 2 to 3 minutes, stirring from time to time. Wash 3 parsley stalks, 1 fresh sprig thyme and 1 bay leaf and tie together to make a bouquet garni, and place in the pan. Add ½ to 1 bottle wine (red or white according to the recipe) and season with salt and pepper. Reduce the wine over high heat for 3 to 5 minutes, then add about 1.5 litres water. Cook, uncovered, over medium heat for about 30 minutes. Strain, squeezing as much liquid as possible from the fish. Reduce further to ½ to ¾ litre stock. Season to taste.

Variation: Matelote à la Lorraine
(Stewed fish Lorraine style)
Instead of using just trout, prepare a mixture of pike-perch, pike and trout (total weight 1 kg cleaned fish) with ¼ litre fish stock, ¼ litre white wine, 250 g crème fraîche, 50 g butter, 1 large shallot, 300 g small mushrooms, salt and pepper, 3 or 4 egg yolks and parsley, following the recipe above.

Truite au bleu à la St.-Roch

Auvergne-style poached trout

More complex • Auvergne

Serves 2

1 large onion
5 cloves
1 small carrot
about 12.5 cl white wine vinegar
salt
8 peppercorns
2 cleaned trout (about 300 g each—see Note)
fresh mint sprigs for garnish

For the sauce à la St.-Roch:
3 to 5 sprigs fresh mint
2 egg yolks • salt
30 to 50 g butter, straight from the refrigerator
freshly ground white pepper
about 1 tsp white wine vinegar

Preparation time: 35 minutes

2,500 kJ/600 calories per portion

1 Peel the onion and spike it with the cloves. Wash, peel and finely chop the carrot. Bring the vegetables to the boil with 2 litres water, 4 tbsp vinegar, salt and peppercorns. Cover and cook over medium heat for 10 to 20 minutes. Wash the trout carefully so the skin is not damaged. Thread a needle with kitchen twine, then pull it through the tail and secure under the gills to curve the fish. Pour over 2 tbsp vinegar.

2 Wash the mint, shake dry and chop finely. Strain the stock. Bring the trout to the boil in the stock, then cover and poach over very low heat for 7 to 10 minutes, until they are cooked through.

3 Meanwhile, make the sauce. Wash the mint, shake it dry and chop it.

Whisk the egg yolks with a little salt in a heatproof bowl set over a pan of hot water until creamy. Remove the bowl from the water and stir small pieces of butter into the yolks until the sauce thickens. Continuing to stir, add more salt, pepper, about 1 tsp vinegar and the chopped mint. Remove the trout from the pan and lay them on a clean cloth. Remove the twine and place the fish on a warmed serving dish. Garnish with the mint. Serve with the sauce.

Note: The traditional French recipe calls for very fresh river trout which are poached in water with a little vinegar, and this turns the skin a soft blue. As river trout are not readily available, you may have to substitute the more common rainbow trout.

Eggs

Eggs are a vital ingredient in French cookery. Some sauces and desserts, however, are prepared with minimal or no cooking, so it is of great importance that the eggs are free of any bacteria that would normally be destroyed by heat.

Eggs are vulnerable to contamination because their shells are porous. The risk is greatly reduced if high standards of cleanliness are practised by the producer; it is always best to buy your eggs from a reliable source.

The use-by date is not always a sound indication of freshness, as eggs may have been laid up to a week before being packed. The bouyancy of eggs increases with age, however, so it is a simple matter to test an egg for freshness. Dissolve about 1 tbsp salt in 1 litre of cold water and add the egg. If it stays on the bottom, the egg is very fresh; if it stands on end, it is still quite fresh; but if it floats to the surface, it is not fresh.

Truites au champagne

Easy • Champagne   **Trout in champagne**   *Serves 4*

about 150 g butter, straight from
the refrigerator
30 g fresh parsley
3 to 5 sprigs fresh thyme
2 cleaned salmon trout (about
550 g each)
salt
ground coriander or white pepper
1 bottle champagne
1 tbsp flour
4 egg yolks
1 tbsp white wine vinegar or juice
of ¼ lemon
1 to 2 tbsp crème fraîche

Preparation time: 55 minutes

3,200 kJ/760 calories per portion

1 Using 15 g of the butter, grease an ovenproof dish, large enough to hold both trout. Preheat the oven to 180°C (350°F or Mark 4). Wash the herbs and shake dry. Tear off the leaves and sprinkle them into the baking dish. Wash the trout and pat dry. Season inside and out with salt and ground coriander, and place in the dish. Melt about 45 g butter over low heat, then pour it all over the fish. Bake in the centre of the oven for about 5 minutes. Pour ¼ litre of the champagne over the fish and return to the oven for another 10 to 15 minutes, basting frequently.

2 To make the sauce, heat 15 g butter in a saucepan. Add the flour and stir over low heat for 1 to 2 minutes, until the roux is lightly browned. Add about ¼ litre champagne and then simmer, uncovered, over low heat for about 10 minutes. Turn off the oven, pour off the fish stock and leave the trout in the oven to keep warm. Strain the fish stock and add it to the sauce. Over high heat, reduce the sauce to 4 tbsp. Mix the egg yolks, vinegar and crème fraîche with 2 to 3 tbsp champagne. Stir the mixture into the sauce. Thinly slice 50 to 70 g butter. Using a hand whisk, gradually beat the butter into the sauce until it becomes smooth and creamy. Season with salt.

3 Carefully push back the skin of the trout with a spoon. Transfer to a warmed serving dish, pour the sauce over the fish and serve.

Féras aux amandes

Simple • Dauphiné

Whitefish with almonds

Serves 4

*4 cleaned, fresh whitefish (see
Glossary) or trout (about
200 g each)*
salt
freshly ground white pepper
2 tbsp flour
1 tbsp vegetable oil
about 45 g butter
40 cl double cream
juice of ½ to 1 lemon
100 g flaked almonds
15 g fresh parsley
1 lemon for garnish

Preparation time: 40 minutes

3,600 kJ/860 calories per portion

1 Preheat the oven to 180°C (350°F or Mark 4). Wash the fish, pat dry and season inside and out with salt and pepper. Dust with flour. Heat the oil and 30 g of the butter in a large frying pan. Fry, uncovered, over high heat for 1 to 2 minutes on each side, until golden-brown, then transfer to a gratin dish. Discard the fat in the pan.

2 Bring the cream to the boil with the juice of half the lemon, and a little salt and pepper. At the same time, heat the frying pan without any fat and stir-fry the almonds over medium heat for not more than 1 minute, until the tips are lightly browned, taking care, as they burn very easily. Remove the pan from the heat and stir in 15 g butter. Pour the cream and almonds over the fish.

Bake in the centre of the oven for 5 to 10 minutes. Season the sauce with the rest of the lemon juice, if liked.

3 Wash the parsley, shake dry and chop finely. Wash and slice the second lemon. Toss the slices in the chopped parsley and use to garnish the fish. Serve immediately, with celeriac purée *(see page 108)* or baguettes.

Variation: Truites grenobloises
(Grenoble-style trout)
Prepare 4 fresh trout as in the recipe above and fry over medium heat for 3 to 4 minutes on each side, until crisp and brown. Sprinkle the cooked trout with the shredded flesh of 2 lemons, 2 tbsp capers, 1 to 2 tbsp chopped fresh parsley and croûtons.

Pauchouse bourguignonne

Fish and white wine stew

Takes time • Burgundy

Serves 4

20 pearl onions or shallots
(2 to 3 cm in diameter)
75 g rindless streaky bacon
6 to 10 garlic cloves
30 g butter
about 1.2 kg freshwater fish
(for example, 1 carp and 1 tench),
cleaned and filleted
¾ litre hot home-made fish stock
(see Note, page 59), made with dry
white wine
salt
freshly ground white pepper
1 tbsp flour
4 to 8 slices coarse rye bread

Preparation time: 1¼ hours
(plus 45 minutes for making the fish
stock, if necessary)

3,100 kJ/740 calories per portion

1 Peel the onions and soak them for 2 to 3 minutes in boiling water, then transfer them to ice-cold water for a further 2 to 3 minutes. Remove from the water and dry thoroughly. Cut the streaky bacon into thin strips.

2 Peel and halve the garlic cloves *(above)*. Heat 15 g of the butter in a frying pan. Reserve 1 garlic clove and fry the rest with the onions and bacon over low heat for about 5 minutes, until the onions are golden-brown.

3 Wash the fish and pat dry. Cut into slices 5 to 6 cm wide; remove any small bones with tweezers *(above)*. Place the fish and the fried onions, bacon and garlic in the hot fish stock. Cover and simmer over very low heat for 10 to 15 minutes. Season with salt and pepper.

4 Using a slotted spoon, carefully transfer the fish, onions, bacon and garlic to a warmed tureen. Knead the flour and remaining butter to make a roux. Bring the sauce to the boil and thicken with the roux. Taste and adjust the seasoning, Pour the boiling hot sauce over the fish.

5 Toast the bread. While still warm, rub the toast with the cut surfaces of the reserved garlic clove. Coarsely dice the toast and sprinkle over the stew. Serve immediately.

Wine: A dry white Burgundy, such as Pernand-Vergelesses, goes well with this fish stew.

Variations: You can also use eel, perch, trout, pike or salmon for this stew. It can be made with ¼ litre dry white wine and water, instead of fish stock. The fish can be flambéed with 2 cl brandy before cooking. If you like a creamy sauce, stir a mixture of the yolk of a fresh egg and 75 g crème fraîche into the sauce at the end of the cooking time. Do not return to the boil.

Meurette de carpes
(Carp stewed in red wine)
For this dish, use 1.2 kg cleaned carp, make the stock with red Burgundy instead of white and add a bouquet garni. The remaining ingredients and the method are the same as for the recipe above.

MEAT

O ne of the best-known and best-loved country dishes, characteristic of the rustic cuisine of eastern France and the Massif Central, is a hearty stew known as *potée*. Nearly always made with pork and vegetables (recipe, page 73), all French *potées* are similar, but there are subtle and delicious distinctions to each one.

Regional meat dishes are prepared with local wines and the same wine used in the sauce is served with the meal. *Vin du pays* is also drunk with everyday dishes, such as those made with offal, sausage and minced meat. The French are exceptionally creative with cheaper cuts of meat.

Large joints of meat are only served on Sundays and feast days. Marinated in wine, the meat is then cooked over low heat or in a very slow oven until it is wonderfully tender and succulent. *Bœuf bourguignon* is one such Sunday speciality. It requires well-aged beef (Burgundians would specify Charolais) and it should be accompanied by a good quality red wine, such as a Côte de Nuits-Villages.

The Easter roast must be lamb or mutton, depending on the size of the family. Particularly popular is *gigot à la sept heures* (recipe variation, page 70), a dish that varies from region to region, but is basically a leg of lamb roasted in a very low oven for seven hours.

Bœuf bourguignon

Beef braised in red wine

Serves 6

1.2 kg silverside or chuck steak
1 large onion
5 cloves
6 to 12 small carrots
1 head of garlic
1 bouquet garni
¾ litre strong red wine (for example, Mercurey)
2 cl brandy
2 tbsp vegetable oil
freshly ground black pepper
250 g pearl onions (2 to 3 cm in diameter)
250 g button mushrooms
100 g rindless streaky bacon
45 g lard or pork fat
salt
1 calf's foot

Preparation time: 40 minutes (plus at least 3 hours' marinating time and 2½ to 3 hours' cooking time)

2,800 kJ/670 calories per portion

1 Wash the meat, pat dry and place in a glass mixing bowl.

2 Peel the large onion and spike with the cloves. Wash and peel the carrots. Leave the garlic head whole, simply rub off the outer skin with your fingers.

3 Add the onion, carrots, garlic and bouquet garni to the meat. Cover with ½ litre of the red wine. Add the brandy and vegetable oil. Season with pepper. Marinate for at least 3 hours, turning the ingredients from time to time.

4 Lift the meat out of the marinade and dry it with paper towels. Strain the marinade. Reserve the liquid, bouquet garni, vegetables and garlic separately.

5 Peel the pearl onions. Briefly rinse or wipe the mushrooms and dry them thoroughly. Trim the stalks and halve or

quarter any large mushrooms. Cut the bacon into strips.

6 Preheat the oven to 110ºC (225ºF or Mark ¼). Heat the lard or pork fat in a large frying pan and fry the bacon over medium heat until crisp and brown, then transfer to a large fireproof casserole or stockpot. Fry the meat in the fat over high heat until crisp and brown all over. Season with salt and pepper. Add to the casserole.

7 Brown the garlic in the fat over low heat for 3 to 5 minutes, then add to the meat. Briefly brown the button onions, carrots and mushrooms in the frying pan, and reserve.

8 Pour off the fat from the frying pan. Add the marinade and cook over high

heat to deglaze the pan. Add the rest of the red wine, heat through and then pour it over the meat.

9 Wash the calf's foot, and add to the casserole, with the bouquet garni and the clove-spiked onion. Season with salt and pepper. Cook on the bottom shelf of the oven for 2½ to 3 hours, adding the pearl onions, carrots and mushrooms about 20 minutes before the end of the cooking time.

10 Strain the sauce. Discard the calf's foot, spiked onion and garlic. Keep the meat and vegetables warm. Skim the fat off the sauce with a spoon. Reduce the sauce over high heat for 5 to 10 minutes, until it thickens, then taste and adjust the seasoning, if necessary.

11 Return the meat and vegetables to the sauce and heat through over low heat for 2 to 3 minutes.

12 Remove the meat, cut it into slices and arrange them on a warmed serving dish. Pour over a little of the sauce and serve the rest separately. Serve the meat with boiled potatoes, creamed potato *(see page 108)* or pasta.

Wine: Serve with the same wine as the one used in the dish: preferably Mercurey or a rich, fruity red from the Côtes-de-Nuits area.

Note: In order to feed a large family, it was customary to braise meat for this dish in joints of more than 2 kg. In more modern recipes, meat for *bœuf bourguignon* is usually cut into cubes.

For a gourmet-style snack, serve the boiled calf's foot with a dressing made with oil, wine vinegar, garlic, chopped shallot and fresh parsley, accompanied by crusty rye bread.

Baeckeoffe

Meat and vegetable casserole

Takes time • Alsace

Serves 4

400 g pork shoulder
400 g boned shoulder of lamb
400 g boned brisket of beef
freshly ground black pepper
250 g onions • 5 garlic cloves
1 bouquet garni
37.5 cl fruity white wine
1.5 kg waxy potatoes
15 g pork dripping or lard
salt • 100 g flour

**Preparation time: 55 minutes
(plus 24 hours' marinating time
and 4 hours' cooking time)**

5,300 kJ/1,300 calories per portion

1 Wash the meat, pat dry, and cut into large, equal-sized pieces. Season with pepper. Peel the onions and cut into rings. Peel the garlic and cut into thin slivers. Place the meat, onions, garlic and bouquet garni in a large bowl. Pour over the wine, cover the bowl and leave to marinate in the refrigerator for about 24 hours.

2 When you are ready to cook, preheat the oven to 150°C (300°F or Mark 2). Peel and slice the potatoes. Grease a large earthenware casserole with the dripping. Remove the meat and onion rings from the marinade, reserving the marinade. Arrange the meat and onions in layers in the casserole, alternating with the potato slices, sprinkling each layer with salt, and ending with a layer of potatoes. Pour the white wine marinade over the top.

3 Mix the flour with 4 to 5 tbsp water to make a dough. Using the palms of your hands, roll the dough into a long strip and place it around the edge of the casserole, then press the lid down firmly so that the casserole is sealed. Cook on the bottom shelf of the oven for about 4 hours. Serve straight from the casserole, accompanied by a salad.

Gigot brayaude

Pot-roasted leg of lamb

Takes time • Auvergne

Serves 6

**2 kg leg of lamb (ask the butcher to
bone the lamb, but keep the bone)**
70 g rindless lean streaky bacon
6 garlic cloves
about 2 tbsp vegetable oil
freshly ground black pepper
400 g onions
200 g carrots
250 g green streaky bacon rashers
about 60 g fat for searing the meat
salt
1 bouquet garni
**37.5 cl dry white wine
(for example, Saint-Pourçain-
sur-Sioule)**

**Preparation time: 1 hour
(plus 24 hours' chilling time and
4 hours' cooking time)**

4,400 kJ/1,000 calories per portion

1 Wash the meat and pat dry. Cut the streaky bacon into thin strips. Peel the garlic. Insert the bacon and garlic between the meat and skin or sinews. Rub the meat with the oil and sprinkle with pepper. Roll up the meat and tie with kitchen twine. Cover and chill in the refrigerator for about 24 hours, removing it 3 hours before cooking.

2 Preheat the oven to 180°C (350°F or Mark 4). Peel the onions, wash and peel the carrots. Slice both vegetables. Line a *daubière* (French earthenware casserole) or roasting pan with half the bacon. Sprinkle the onions and carrots on top. Heat the fat in a large frying pan and sear the lamb on all sides over high heat for 10 minutes. Season with salt. Transfer the meat to the *daubière* or roasting pan with the bone, bouquet garni and wine. Cover with the rest of the bacon and place on the bottom shelf of the oven. Cook for about 30 minutes, then reduce the oven temperature to the minimum and continue to cook for about 3½ hours. Turn off the heat and leave to stand in the oven for about 10 minutes.

3 Strain the sauce and skim off the fat, then boil over high heat to reduce to about ¼ litre. Remove the twine and carve the meat into slices. Arrange on a warm dish and pour over the sauce.

Variation: Gigot à la sept heures
(Seven-hour leg of lamb)
Do all the cooking for this lamb dish at minimum temperature in the oven—this will take about 7 hours, depending on how low your oven will go.

Pot-au-feu de bœuf gros sel

Boiled beef and vegetables with coarse salt

Takes time • Lorraine

Serves 6 to 8

2 kg stewing beef (for example, silverside or flank on the bone)
2 onions • 8 cloves • 2 garlic cloves
4 bay leaves • 20 peppercorns
dried thyme • salt
2 small savoy cabbages
4 carrots • 4 white turnips
½ celeriac • 2 leeks
8 medium-sized waxy potatoes
coarse salt
100 g ready-made horseradish
500 g pickled beetroot

Preparation time: 50 minutes
(plus 2 hours' cooking time)

2,200 kJ/520 calories per portion
(if serving 8)

1 Wash the meat. Peel the onions and spike them with the cloves (the onions can be browned in the oven first for a stronger flavour, if wished). Peel the garlic. Place the meat, onions, garlic, bay leaves, peppercorns and a little thyme in a large, heavy saucepan or stockpot with 3 to 4 litres cold water. Bring to the boil over high heat, then add salt. Partly cover with the lid and simmer over low heat for 2 hours.

2 Meanwhile, wash and trim all the vegetables. Cut both the cabbages into quarters. Halve the carrots and turnips crosswise. Cut the celeriac into eight wedges. Cut the leeks into four pieces. Peel the potatoes and cook in boiling salted water for 20 minutes. Remove the meat from the broth. Strain the broth through a sieve and skim the fat from the surface. Simmer the cabbage, carrots, turnips, leeks and celeriac in the broth over low heat for 15 to 20 minutes. Season with salt and pepper. Detach the meat from the bones and heat it in the broth for 3 to 5 minutes.

3 Reserve one large ladleful of the broth, then serve the remainder as a first course. Cut the meat into slices and arrange on a warmed serving dish, surrounded by the cooked vegetables. Pour the reserved broth over the top. Sprinkle with coarse salt. Serve with horseradish and pickled beetroot.

Potée des vendangeurs

Grape-pickers' stew

Not difficult • Champagne

Serves 6 to 8

350 g dried white haricot beans
1 cured pork knuckle
1 ready-cleaned boiling fowl (about 1.5 kg)
800 g smoked belly of pork
400 g medium-sized waxy potatoes
4 carrots • 4 white turnips
1 white or savoy cabbage (about 1 kg)
600 g boiling sausage
freshly ground black pepper
crusty rye bread for serving

Preparation time: 45 minutes
(plus 12 hours' soaking time and 2½ hours' cooking time)

6,500 kJ/1,500 calories per portion
(if serving 8)

1 Cover the beans with cold water and soak overnight. Soak the pork knuckle in plenty of water for about 12 hours to remove the salt, changing the water frequently during that time.

2 Wash the pork knuckle, boiling fowl and belly of pork, and place in a very large saucepan or stockpot. Add 3 to 4 litres cold water and bring to the boil over high heat. Cover and simmer over low heat for about 1½ hours. Remove the belly of pork and reserve. Drain the beans and add to the pan. Cook for another 30 minutes.

3 Wash and peel the potatoes, carrots and turnips, then halve the carrots and turnips. Trim and wash the cabbage and cut into eight wedges. Add the vegetables and boiling sausage to the broth and cook for another 30 minutes. Return the belly of pork to the pot and heat through briefly. Skim the fat from the surface. Season with pepper.

4 Transfer the vegetables, meat and sausage to a large tureen and pour over 1 to 2 ladlefuls of broth. Keep warm. Serve the remaining broth as a first course, then serve the sausage, meat and vegetables with rye bread.

Wine: This stew, designed to sustain hard-working grape-pickers and ideal for a Sunday lunch, is best served with a fruity red wine, such as Bouzy Rouge from the Champagne district.

Tournedos Dijonnaise

Fillet steak with mustard sauce

Quick • Burgundy

Serves 2

2 tbsp vegetable oil
30 g butter
2 tournedos steaks (about 200 g each), wrapped in bacon rashers or fat by the butcher
2 tbsp brandy (for example, Fine Bourgogne)
salt
freshly ground black pepper
1 heaped tsp Dijon mustard
10 cl double cream
2 thick slices white bread
sugar (optional)
few parsley sprigs for garnish

Preparation time: 10 minutes

2,500 kJ/600 calories per portion

1 Heat the oil and butter in a frying pan and fry the tournedos steaks for about 2 minutes on each side. (If you do not like steak pink in the middle, fry for 4 to 5 minutes on each side.) Pour off the fat in the pan. Warm the brandy in a ladle over the pan, then pour it over the steaks and ignite it.

2 Season the steaks to taste with salt and pepper, remove them from the pan and wrap first in foil, then in a towel and leave to stand for about 5 minutes.

3 Meanwhile, stir the Dijon mustard and cream into the pan juices and cook over high heat until reduced to 2 tbsp. Trim the bread slices to the same size as the steaks and toast on both sides.

4 Unwrap the steaks and stir the meat juices that have collected in the foil into the sauce. Season with salt, pepper and sugar to taste. Arrange the toast on warmed plates, place a steak on top of each round of toast. Pour over the sauce, garnish with parsley and serve immediately.

Wine: A three- or four-year-old red Burgundy, such as Beaune or Volnay, goes well with *tournedos dijonnaise.*

Variation: Tournedos sauce Roquefort (Fillet steak with Roquefort sauce) Prepare 2 thick fillet steaks as above, omitting the bacon. To make Roquefort sauce, reduce 10 cl double cream to 2 tbsp, add 50 g Roquefort cheese, and stir until the cheese has melted.

Charolais cattle

Charolais, in southern Burgundy, owes its fame chiefly to the breed of beef cattle of the same name. With their distinctive light colour, the cattle stand out from a distance as tiny patches of white against the endless green pastures.

Charolais cattle are one of France's most popular beef cattle breeds. They are still reared today in the time-honoured way, spending most of their life grazing in the meadows, and this gives their meat its incomparable flavour. Quality is guaranteed by the *Label Rouge* (red label): few would dare to abuse the certifying authority of the "Association for the defence of traditional breeding of Charolais beef".

Like tender, succulent meat in general, Charolais beef has an attractive, almost shiny, dark reddish colour, and is well marbled by a fine network of white or pale yellow fat. It should be firm and elastic to the touch, and have a barely detectable, but pleasant, slightly sweet smell. Quality depends on the age, sex and diet of the animal, as well as the time of year when it is slaughtered. The cows' meat is generally inferior to that of young bullocks.

Pounti

Swiss chard pudding

Easy • Auvergne

Serves 4

lard for greasing
300 g Swiss chard or spinach
250 g prunes with stones
1 to 2 tbsp raisins
15 g fresh parsley
15 g fresh chervil
200 g lean smoked belly of pork
2 large onions
1 to 2 garlic cloves
2 tbsp flour
10 cl milk
3 eggs
salt
freshly ground black pepper
fresh sprigs chervil for garnish
(optional)

Preparation time: 1 hour
(plus 1 hour's cooking time)

2,400 kJ/570 calories per portion

1 Preheat the oven to 150°C (300°F or Mark 2). Grease a round 24 cm gratin dish. Wash the Swiss chard or spinach and blanch it in boiling water for about 3 minutes. Rinse in ice-cold water and drain thoroughly in a colander. Wash the prunes and raisins. Wash the herbs and shake dry. Pat the ingredients dry.

2 With a knife or food processor, finely chop the belly of pork. Peal and finely chop the onions and garlic. Coarsely chop the raisins. Finely chop the chard and herbs separately

3 In a bowl, mix the flour, milk and eggs to a batter, stirring to remove any lumps. Mix all the chopped ingredients into the batter, season with salt and pepper, and stir in the prunes.

4 Pour the mixture into the dish and bake on the bottom shelf of the oven for about 1 hour, until golden-brown.

5 Cut the pudding into portions in the dish (watching out for prune stones). Garnish with sprigs of chervil, if liked, and serve piping hot.

Wine: A Côtes-d'Auvergne, a rosé or red wine from the Clermont-Ferrand district, is perfect with this country-style dish.

Variations:
Pounti, which started out as an Auvergne peasant dish, can also be made as a vegetarian dish by omitting the pork, if wished.

Pountari (Pork sausage)
To serve 6 to 8 people, prepare the pudding mixture as described in the recipe, then stuff loosely into a large sausage skin. Stitch together with kitchen twine, then simmer, covered, in 2 litres of vegetable broth for about 35 minutes. It will swell considerably while cooking. Slice the *pountari* and serve in the vegetable broth.

Truffado (Potato cake with bacon and Cantal cheese)
To serve 4 people, peel and slice 6 waxy potatoes. Cut 12 rashers rindless streaky bacon into wide strips. Fry the bacon in a frying pan with 45 g lard or pork dripping until crisp. Add the potato slices and brown over medium heat for 2 to 3 minutes. Season with pepper, then top with 150 g sliced Cantal cheese (or another mild cow's milk cheese). Cover the pan and cook over low heat for 30 to 45 minutes.

Note: *Truffado* is the staple diet of the herdsmen who spend 3 to 4 summer months living in *burons* (alpine huts) in the mountains of the Auvergne, producing Cantal cheese. These old-fashioned recipes are now heartily enjoyed by the rest of the population.

Gratin savoyard et diots

Takes time • Savoy

Potato gratin with sausages in wine sauce

Serves 4 to 6

For the gratin:
1 garlic clove • 50 g butter
8 waxy potatoes (about 1 kg)
salt • freshly ground black pepper
freshly grated nutmeg
250 g freshly grated Beaufort or
Gruyère cheese
½ litre warm chicken stock (see
Note, page 38)

For the sausages in wine sauce:
16 diots (short pork sausages) or
600 g pork sausages
60 g butter • 2 medium-sized onions
4 shallots • 1 tbsp flour
¼ litre white wine
1 bouquet garni
3 to 5 sprigs fresh parsley

Preparation time: 1½ hours
(plus 1½ hours for making the
stock, if necessary)

3,300 kJ/790 calories per portion
(if serving 6)

1 Peel and halve the garlic clove, then rub a large gratin dish with the cut surface of the garlic and grease with 15 g butter. Preheat the oven to 180°C (350°F or Mark 4). Wash, peel and thinly slice the potatoes. Soak in cold water for 1 to 2 minutes, then remove and pat dry. Arrange a layer of potato slices in the bottom of the gratin dish. Sprinkle with salt, pepper, nutmeg and about a quarter of the grated cheese. Repeat the layers once or twice more, sprinkling each layer with seasonings and grated cheese. Pour the warm stock over the potatoes. Sprinkle with the rest of the cheese and flake the remaining butter on top. Bake in the centre of the oven for 30 minutes.

2 Meanwhile, prepare the sausages. Prick their skins with a needle. Heat 30 g butter in a frying pan and brown the sausages over high heat for 2 to 3 minutes, then fry for 10 minutes over low heat, turning from time to time.

3 Peel and halve the onions and the shallots, and cut into 5 mm slices. Heat the remaining butter in a pan and sauté the onions and shallots for about 5 minutes, until transparent. Sprinkle with the flour, add the wine, cover and simmer over low heat for 10 minutes. Season with salt and pepper. Add the sausages and bouquet garni, re-cover and simmer over low heat for about 20 minutes. Discard the bouquet garni.

4 Strain the sauce through a coarse sieve. Remove the gratin from the oven and increase the oven temperature to 250°C (450°F or Mark 8). Pour off the stock from the gratin dish (it can be used for soup). Spread the onions and shallots remaining in the sieve over the gratin. Bake at the top of the oven for 5 to 10 minutes, until crisp and brown. Wash the parsley, shake dry and tear off the leaves. Arrange the sausages on top of the gratin, sprinkle with parsley and serve with the sauce.

Saucisson, pommes à l'huile

Simple • Lyonnais

Hot sausages with potato salad

Serves 4

600 g small, new, waxy potatoes
4 Lyonnais sausages or pork boiling
sausages (150 g each)
30 g fresh chives
6 tbsp olive oil
3 tbsp wine vinegar
3 tbsp white wine
salt • freshly ground black pepper

Preparation time: 40 minutes

3,100 kJ/710 calories per portion

1 Wash the potatoes, then cook them in their skins in boiling salted water for 10 to 15 minutes over medium heat. Drain the potatoes and leave to steam and cool a little.

2 Meanwhile, place the sausages in a saucepan and cover with cold water. Bring slowly to the boil, cover the pan and simmer the sausages over low heat for about 20 minutes. Leave them in the water to keep warm.

3 Wash the chives, shake, then pat dry and snip into thin rings. Mix the olive oil, vinegar and white wine to make a dressing. Season with salt and pepper.

4 Peel the warm potatoes and toss in a bowl with the dressing. Sprinkle the salad with the chopped chives.

5 Cut the sausages in half lengthwise, then slice thickly. Serve them with the warm potato salad.

Cervelle d'agneau meurette

Lamb's brains in red wine sauce

Easy • Burgundy   *Serves 2*

4 lambs' brains (about 100 g each)
1 medium-sized onion
1 garlic clove
1 carrot
1 bouquet garni
¼ litre red Burgundy
salt
freshly ground black pepper
sugar
juice of ¼ lemon
about 75 g butter, straight from the refrigerator
1 egg yolk
4 slices white bread

Preparation time: 40 minutes (plus about 1 hour's soaking time)

3,400 kJ/810 calories per portion

1 Rinse the brains, then place them in a bowl, cover with lukewarm water and leave to soak for about 1 hour, changing the water several times. Peel the onion and garlic. Wash the carrot. Finely chop the onion, garlic and carrot. Bring the vegetables, bouquet garni and wine to the boil in a small saucepan, then cover and simmer over medium heat for about 10 minutes. Season to taste with salt, pepper and a little sugar.

2 Pour off the water from the brains. Cover with ½ litre boiling water and sprinkle with the lemon juice. Leave to stand for 1 to 2 minutes, then plunge the brains into ice-cold water, remove and pat dry. Add them to the red wine sauce and simmer over low heat for about 5 minutes. Remove the brains from the pan and keep warm.

3 Strain the sauce, squeezing all the liquid from the vegetables. Return the sauce to the pan and boil over high heat until reduced to about 12.5 cl. Flake in 50 g of the butter to bind the sauce. Remove from the heat and stir in the egg yolk. Season with salt and pepper. Return the brains to the sauce and keep warm.

4 Cut the bread into small cubes and toast in a frying pan without fat, until golden-brown. Remove the pan from the heat and add the rest of the butter. Toss the bread in the melted butter. Serve the brains on warmed plates, covered with the sauce and sprinkled with the croûtons.

Wine: Serve the brains with the wine that you use to make the sauce. A dry red from one of the villages around Beaune would be ideal.

Côte de porc à l'Arboisienne

Easy • Franche-Comté   **Arbois-style pork chops**   *Serves 4*

½ **litre milk**
about 75 g **butter**
1 tbsp **flour**
1 **bay leaf**
salt
100 g freshly grated **Comté** or
Gruyère cheese
freshly grated **nutmeg**
4 **pork chops** (about 250 g each)
freshly ground **black pepper**
¼ litre **white wine** (for example,
Arbois)
2 **garlic cloves**
4 thick slices coarse **rye bread**
sprigs fresh **parsley** for garnish

Preparation time: 40 minutes

3,900 kJ/930 calories per portion

1 Heat the milk in a saucepan. Melt 15 g of the butter in a separate small pan. Stir in the flour and cook over low heat until the roux is lightly browned. Stir in the milk a little at a time. Add the bay leaf and a little salt. Cover and simmer the sauce over low heat for about 20 minutes, then discard the bay leaf. Stir half the grated cheese into the sauce and season to taste with salt and grated nutmeg.

2 Meanwhile, preheat the oven to 180°C (350°F or Mark 4). Season the pork chops with a little pepper. Heat 30 g butter in a frying pan and brown the chops over medium heat for 2 to 3 minutes on each side. Season with salt. Grease a roasting pan with the rest of the butter. Add the chops. Pour off the fat in the frying pan. Pour the wine into the pan and cook over high heat to

deglaze the pan and reduce the wine to 2 tbsp, then sprinkle it over the chops. Bake in the centre of the oven for 10 to 15 minutes, until cooked through. Remove from the oven. Increase the oven temperature to 250°C (450°F or Mark 8).

3 Pour the cheese sauce over the chops and sprinkle with the rest of the cheese. Return the chops to the oven for about 3 minutes, until the cheese is melted and golden. Meanwhile, peel and halve the garlic. Toast the bread slices until crisp and rub with the cut surfaces of the garlic.

4 Arrange the garlic bread on four warmed plates and place one chop on top of each slice. Garnish with parsley.

Gras-double comtoise

Tripe in vinegar and cream sauce

3 large onions
9 cloves
6 carrots (about 175 g)
1 bouquet garni
salt
freshly ground black pepper
1 kg dressed tripe, ordered in advance from the butcher
4 medium-sized potatoes (about 400 g)
5 shallots
100 g butter
10 to 12.5 cl red wine vinegar
375 to 500 g crème fraîche
15 g parsley

Preparation time: 1½ hours (plus 1½ to 2 hours' cooking time)

4,100 kJ/980 calories per portion

1 Peel the onions and spike them with the cloves. Wash and peel the carrots. Bring the onions, carrots and bouquet garni to the boil with 2 litres of water. Season with salt and pepper. Add the tripe, cover and simmer over low heat for 1½ to 2 hours, until tender. Top up with more water, if necessary, so that the tripe is always covered. Drain the tripe, reserving the stock. Discard the onions and bouquet garni. Leave the carrots to cool slightly, then cut them into thick slices, and reserve.

2 Pat the tripe dry and leave to cool, then cut it into strips about 5 mm wide *(above)*.

3 Wash and peel the potatoes and cut them into small dice. Cook, covered, in 1 litre of the tripe stock over medium heat for 15 to 20 minutes, then drain.

4 Peel and coarsely chop the shallots. Melt 30 g of the butter in a pan and sauté the shallots, covered, over low heat for 5 to 10 minutes until they are transparent. Add the vinegar and boil until reduced to 1 to 2 tbsp, taking care that the mixture does not burn. Add the crème fraîche and season with salt and pepper. Rub the sauce through a sieve. Add the sliced carrots to the sauce and keep warm.

5 Heat 30 g of the remaining butter in a large frying pan over medium heat until frothy. Fry the tripe in batches over high heat for 2 to 3 minutes, until the strips are lightly browned, adding a little more butter to the pan for each batch. Add the tripe to the carrots in the hot sauce and stir in the potatoes.

6 Wash the parsley, shake it dry and tear off the leaves. Transfer the tripe to a serving dish and serve garnished with the parsley.

Wine: Arbois-Pupillin, a light rosé or red wine from the Jura, is good with this tripe dish and also with various summertime dishes.

Note: The French love offal. Tripe is a mainstay of home cooking. Since tripe has very little taste of its own, it can be combined with all sorts of other ingredients whose flavour it absorbs. The thinner you cut the strips of tripe, the better it tastes.

Variation: Tripes aux morilles
(Tripe in morel sauce)
Use the same ingredients and method as in the recipe above, but cook the tripe in water and white wine (half and half). Reserve the cooked carrot slices and use them for another dish. Moisten the chopped shallots with the juice of 1 lemon instead of the wine vinegar. Cook 60 g fresh morels, uncovered, in ¼ litre water over high heat for about 10 minutes *(see page 38)*. Add the cooked morels and tripe to the sauce and heat through.

GAME AND POULTRY

Eastern France and the Massif Central have only modest stocks of game. Roe deer are native to Alsace and pheasants to Lorraine. Hares are found in Burgundy, Franche-Comté, Savoy and Dauphiné, while the Auvergne is home to wild boar, pigeons and partridge.

Each family has its favourite game recipes for special meals at Christmas and New Year. Goose liver, wine, cognac, truffles and crème fraîche are classic ingredients in these festive game dishes, while chestnut purée is a traditional accompaniment. A good red wine always accompanies such special meals.

Poultry, on the other hand, is in plentiful supply. Many farmers in these regions produce excellent free-range poultry, but Bresse is the bastion of the poultry industry, rearing the only birds to carry a certificate of quality like a fine wine—and command correspondingly high prices. Regional chicken specialities are prepared with lots of fresh butter and cream. Local variations include the addition of morels, truffles and wine.

Goose and turkey are top of the list when it comes to celebratory meals. In Alsace, "St Martin's goose" is served to mark the saint's day on 11 November. And without turkey, Christmas dinner would not be the same in France. Each region has its own way of preparing roast turkey in all its splendour, surrounded by delicious trimmings.

Pigeonneau aux lentilles

Not difficult • Auvergne **Pigeons with green lentils**

Serves 4

**2 pigeons with giblets (see Note),
cleaned and trimmed**

salt

**100 g rindless fatty bacon, in one
piece (ask the butcher to cut off 2
thin rashers)**

**400 g green or brown lentils (for
example, Puy lentils)**

1 medium-sized onion

3 cloves

3 medium-sized carrots

2 bouquets garnis

mineral water

freshly ground black pepper

1 to 2 garlic cloves

2 shallots

**¼ litre fruity white wine (for
example, Saint-Pourçain)**

**30 g fresh parsley, washed and
chopped (optional)**

Preparation time: 1½ hours

3,600 kJ/860 calories per portion

1 Wash the pigeons and giblets, and pat dry with paper towels. Season the insides of the pigeons with a little salt. Sprinkle the livers with salt and place them inside the birds. Lay a rasher of bacon across the breast of each bird and truss with kitchen twine *(above)*.

2 Wash the lentils. Peel the onion and spike it with the cloves. Wash the carrots. Place the lentils in a saucepan with the rest of the giblets, the onion, 1 carrot and 1 bouquet garni. Cover with mineral water and season lightly with salt and pepper. Bring to the boil over high heat, then cover the pan and simmer over low heat for 45 minutes. Top up with more water, if necessary, to keep the lentils covered.

3 Meanwhile, dice the rest of the bacon and fry in a frying pan over high heat until the fat runs. Fry the pigeons in the bacon fat over medium heat for 5 to 8 minutes, until crisp and brown. Remove from the pan and season with salt. Peel the garlic and shallots, trim the remaining carrots. Finely chop the vegetables and brown them in the fat over medium heat. Drain off the fat and add the wine to the pan.

4 Add the birds, breast upwards, and second bouquet garni to the vegetables in the pan. Cover and braise over low

heat for 30 minutes, basting frequently with the pan juices. Leave the pigeons to rest in the hot pan for 10 minutes.

5 Remove the bouquet garni, onion, carrot and giblets from the lentil pan. Strain the pan juices from the pigeons and the vegetables through a sieve, squeezing the juice from the cooked vegetables. Stir the juices into the lentils, using a wooden spoon and taking care not to break up the lentils.

6 Remove the bacon and twine from the pigeons. Pour the lentils into a warmed oval serving dish. Stuff the body cavities of the pigeons with the parsley, if using. Arrange the birds on top of the lentils *(above)* and serve immediately.

Note: Young, tender pigeons, specially bred for the table, and often called squabs, have light reddish flesh with a good flavour. They are more expensive than wood pigeons.

**Variation: Estouffade de perdrix
aux lentilles du Puy**
(Partridge with Puy lentils)
Use the same method as above, but cook 2 partridges (about 500 g each) for 1½ hours. This dish is served in France during the hunting season from mid-October to 1 January.

Médaillon de biche

Medallions of venison with cranberry sauce

Serves 2

**2 medallions of venison (about
150 g each), ordered in advance
from the butcher
freshly ground black pepper
30 g butter
2 tbsp vegetable oil
2 cl kirsch
salt
3 tbsp cranberry sauce (from a jar)
1 tbsp grated horseradish (from
a jar)**

Preparation time: 20 minutes

1,800 kJ/430 calories per portion

1 Preheat a serving dish in the oven at 150°C (300°F or Mark 2). Season the meat with pepper. Heat the butter and oil in a frying pan, and fry the meat for 2 to 4 minutes on each side, until golden-brown. Pour the kirsch into a ladle, warm through briefly over the edge of the pan, then pour it over the venison. Carefully ignite the kirsch and flambé the meat.

2 Remove the meat from the pan and season with salt. Wrap immediately in aluminium foil and then in a tea towel. Pour off the fat from the pan.

3 Add the cranberry sauce to the pan and heat over low heat. Stir in the horseradish and season to taste with salt and pepper.

4 Unwrap the meat and place it on the warmed serving dish. Stir the juices that have collected in the foil into the sauce. Pour the sauce over the venison and serve immediately, accompanied by warm individual brioches straight from the oven or *gratin dauphinois (see Variation, below)*.

Wine: In Alsace, game is served with dry, fruity, red wine from the same region, such as Pinot Noir.

Variation: Escalopes de chevreuil au gratin dauphinois
(Escalopes of venison with potato gratin)
To make a potato gratin for 4, bring ½ litre milk to the boil, uncovered, in a deep saucepan with 2 to 3 peeled and chopped garlic cloves, 2 cloves, a little dried thyme and salt. Boil the mixture over medium heat until reduced to

about ¼ litre, then strain through a sieve. Wash and peel 4 waxy potatoes (about 600 g) and cut into thin (about 3 mm) slices. Add the potatoes to the milk, with salt and pepper and 20 cl double cream. Return to the boil over medium heat, stirring constantly, until the sliced potatoes are thoroughly coated with cream.

Peel 1 garlic glove and 1 white turnip. Rub four small gratin dishes with the garlic and turnip then grease with butter. Divide the potatoes between the four dishes and bake in the oven at 180°C (350°F or Mark 4) for 25 to 35 minutes, until golden-brown.

Season 4 venison escalopes (about 150 g each) with pepper. Heat 45 g butter and 3 tbsp oil in a frying pan and sear the escalopes over high heat for 3 to 5 minutes on each side. Season with salt, remove from the pan and keep warm.

Pour off the fat from the pan and add 10 cl red wine to deglaze the pan. Add 2 tbsp double cream and reduce the sauce to 4 to 6 tbsp over medium heat. Season with salt and pepper. Place each gratin dish on a saucer and serve separately with the meat and sauce.

Never include eggs or cheese in a *gratin dauphinois*. This speciality is served with refined dishes which do not go well with cheese. The white turnip is the real secret of authentic *gratin dauphinois*, which should never be confused with *gratin savoyard (see page 79)*. Serve Crozes-Hermitage, a red wine from the Rhône Valley on the edge of the Val d'Isère in Dauphiné, with game and *gratin dauphinois*.

Rôti de chevreuil à la royale

Royal roast venison *Serves 4 to 6*

For the marinade:
1 carrot
1 stick celery
2 shallots
3 to 5 garlic cloves
¾ litre fruity red wine (for example, Pinot Noir)
1 tsp red wine vinegar
2 tbsp vegetable oil
2 cl brandy
1 bouquet garni
10 juniper berries
10 black peppercorns
3 cloves
freshly grated nutmeg

For the meat:
1 kg rolled haunch of venison
(order in advance and ask the butcher to wrap the joint in bacon)
1 tbsp vegetable oil
15 g butter
salt
freshly ground black pepper
6 tbsp double cream
50 to 100 g finely chopped goose liver (optional)

**Preparation time: 1 hour
(plus 3 days' marinating time)**

**1,700 kJ/400 calories per portion
(if serving 6)**

1 Wash and trim the carrot and celery. Peel the shallots. Peel and halve the garlic. Chop all the vegetables. Mix the wine, carrot, celery, shallots, garlic, vinegar, oil, brandy, bouquet garni and spices in a bowl. Briefly rinse the meat under cold running water, pat dry and place in the marinade. Cover the bowl and leave to marinate for three days in the refrigerator, turning the joint of meat twice a day.

2 Take the meat out of the refrigerator at least 2 hours before starting to cook it. Remove the joint from the marinade and pat dry with paper towels. Reserve the marinade.

3 Preheat the oven to 200°C (400°F or Mark 6). Heat the oil and butter in a frying pan and sear the meat over high heat for 5 to 8 minutes, until browned all round. Season with salt and pepper. Remove the meat from the pan and pour off the fat. Bring the marinade to the boil in the frying pan, then strain and reserve. Transfer the vegetables, spices and herbs from the sieve to a roasting pan and place the meat on top. Roast the joint in the centre of the oven for about 10 minutes, sprinkling frequently with the marinade, 1 tbsp at a time. Turn off the heat and leave the meat to rest in the oven, with the door closed, for a further 20 minutes. (The venison will be deliciously tender and pink inside. If you do not like the meat pink, roast it for 15 to 20 minutes.)

4 Rub the pan juices through a sieve, add to the rest of the marinade, then reduce to about 33 cl over high heat. Add the double cream and cook until the sauce is smooth and creamy.

5 Stir in the chopped goose liver, if using, to bind the sauce. Remove the sauce from the heat immediately, as it curdles very quickly. Season to taste with salt and pepper and keep warm over a bain-marie.

6 Remove the twine from the joint. Carve the meat into equal-sized slices and arrange on a warmed serving dish. Drizzle 2 tbsp sauce over the meat and serve the rest separately. Serve with chestnut purée *(see page 104)* and wild mushrooms *(page 56)*. Celeriac purée *(page 108)* or *gratin dauphinois (page 89)* can also be served with roast venison.

Wine: Serve the same wine as you have used for the marinade, preferably a fruity red Pinot Noir from Alsace.

Variation: Gigot d'agneau
(Leg of lamb in Burgundy wine)
Marinate a leg of lamb on the bone (1.8 to 2 kg to serve 6) for three days, using the same marinade ingredients as for roast venison, but using a red Burgundy instead of Alsace wine. Sear the lamb in the same way as the venison, then cook, uncovered, in the oven at 200°C (400°F or Mark 6) for about 30 minutes. Leave the meat to rest in the cooling oven for a further 15 minutes. Bind the sauce with 30 to 60 g slivered butter straight from the refrigerator. Add a few green or red peppercorns from a jar. Serve with *gratin dauphinois (see page 89)*.

Dinde rôtie

Roast turkey

Not difficult • Auvergne

Serves 6 to 8

1 oven-ready turkey (about 3 kg)
salt
freshly ground black pepper
about 30 g butter, at room
temperature
½ to ¾ litre chicken or turkey stock
(see Note, page 38)
10 cl double cream

Preparation time: 3 hours
(plus 1½ hours for making the
stock, if necessary)

3,800 kJ/900 calories per portion
(if serving 8)

1 Preheat the oven to 180°C (350°F or Mark 4). Wash the turkey and pat dry. Season inside and out with salt and pepper. Place the turkey in a roasting pan. Spread the butter over it and pour over ¼ litre of the stock. Roast in the centre of the oven for about 2½ hours, until golden-brown, basting frequently with the rest of the stock.

2 Turn off the oven and leave the roast turkey to rest for about 10 minutes in the oven, with the door half-open. Strain the pan juices and skim off the fat. Pour the juices into a saucepan, add the cream and reduce over high heat to about 33 cl.

3 Carve the turkey at the table, and serve with the sauce and savoy cabbage with apples, prunes and chestnuts *(see variation, page 107)*.

Wine: Roast turkey can be served with a white, red or rosé wine, such as a Saint-Pourçain from the Auvergne.

Variation: Dinde farcie
(Stuffed turkey)
To make the stuffing, brown 100 g diced, rindless, streaky bacon in 15 to 30 g goose fat. Add 2 peeled and finely chopped shallots, 2 peeled garlic cloves, 200 g chopped chicken liver and the turkey liver cut into strips. Fry for a further 2 minutes. Stir in 400 g mixed minced meat, 1 egg, 2 tbsp crème fraîche and 100 g stoned and chopped prunes. Season with salt and pepper. Stuff the turkey, sew up the body cavity with kitchen twine, or secure with wooden toothpicks. Cook according to the recipe above, but roast for about 30 minutes longer.

Oie à l'Alsacienne

Alsatian goose

Takes time • Alsace

Serves 6 to 8

1 oven-ready goose (about 4 kg)
salt
freshly ground black pepper
3 large cooking apples (for example, reinette)
½ litre goose or chicken stock (see Note, page 38)
6 to 8 thin rashers rindless streaky bacon
6 to 8 chipolata sausages
30 g goose fat

Preparation time: 2¾ hours (plus 1½ hours for making the stock, if necessary)

6,200 kJ/1,500 calories per portion (if serving 8)

1 Preheat the oven to 200°C (400°F or Mark 6). Wash the goose, pat dry and season it inside and out with salt and pepper. Wash, quarter and core the apples, then stuff the goose with them. Tie the legs together with kitchen twine, and secure the body cavity with wooden toothpicks.

2 Place the goose, breast upwards, in a roasting pan. Pour ¼ litre stock over the goose and roast on the bottom shelf of the oven for about 30 minutes. Reduce the oven temperature to 180°C (350°F or Mark 4) and cook the goose for a further 1¾ hours, basting frequently with the pan juices. When cooked, turn off the heat and leave to rest in the cooling oven with the door half-open for 10 to 15 minutes. Transfer the goose to a serving dish and keep warm. Using a ladle, skim the fat from the pan juices. Add the rest of

the stock and reduce over high heat until the sauce is smooth.

3 Wrap the bacon rashers around the chipolatas and secure with wooden toothpicks. Heat the goose fat and fry the chipolatas for about 5 minutes, until crisp and brown all round. Serve the goose garnished with the chipolatas, and accompanied by Alsace sauerkraut *(see page 107)* and boiled or creamed potatoes *(see page 108)*.

Wine: A Riesling or Sylvaner from Alsace is excellent with roast goose.

Variation: Replace the cooking apples with sausage meat stuffing, using four times the quantities given on page 35.

Poulet au vin jaune

Easy • Franche-Comté **Chicken with Jura wine** **Serves 4**

250 g fresh or 25 to 40 g dried morels
1 oven-ready chicken (preferably a Bresse chicken, about 1.6 kg) or 4 chicken joints (350 g each)
salt
freshly ground black pepper
200 g butter
50 g shallots
12.5 cl vin jaune (see Glossary) or 4 cl sherry and 8 cl white wine
about 100 g plain flour
50 cl double cream

Preparation time: 1½ hours (plus up to 2 hours' soaking time, if using dried morels)

4,700 kJ/1,100 calories per portion

1 If using dried morels, soak them for 1 to 2 hours in ¼ litre lukewarm water. Wash fresh morels thoroughly.

2 Preheat the oven to 180°C (350°F or Mark 4). Wash the chicken, pat dry and divide into four joints. Season with salt and pepper. Heat the butter in a frying pan. Fry the joints over medium heat for 8 to 10 minutes, without browning. Peel and chop the shallots. Transfer 3 tbsp fat from the frying pan to a fireproof casserole or a stockpot and briefly fry the shallots. Add the vin jaune and chicken joints.

3 Knead the flour with 4 to 5 tbsp water to a dough. Using the palms of your hands, roll the dough into a long strip and lay it around the edge of the casserole or stockpot lid. Press the lid down firmly so that the casserole is hermetically sealed. Cook in the centre of the oven for 40 to 50 minutes.

4 Cook the morels in ¼ litre water (either the strained soaking water or fresh), uncovered, over high heat, until all the liquid has evaporated. Strain the juices from the frying pan and pour into another pan with the cream. Boil the sauce over high heat until it is reduced to about ¼ litre. Season with salt and pepper. Pour the sauce over the chicken and serve with creamed potatoes *(see page 108)* or croûtons.

Bresse chickens

The Bresse district lies east of Lyonnais and south of Burgundy, and while it produces many fine foods, its greatest claim to fame is its free-range poultry. Bresse chickens are held by many to be, quite simply, the best in the world. They are the only chickens to carry an official AOC (Appellation d'Origine Contrôlée), the same certificate of quality and origin awarded to good French wines.

Bresse chickens are easily recognizable by their snowy white plumage, blue legs and red crest. They are typically very healthy, disease-free birds, a fact which must be largely attributable to their superior diet and method of rearing.

When they are thirty-five days old, Bresse chickens are allowed to run free for about nine weeks. For the last eight to fifteen days before they are slaughtered, the chickens are fattened on dairy products, maize and cereal.

They may only be killed for the table when they are at least four months old and weigh no less than 1.5 kg.

Brillat-Savarin, the French gastronome, wrote that "When fattened, the birds of Bresse are to cuisine what canvas is to painters".

Poulet aux écrevisses

Chicken with crayfish

Takes time • Dauphiné

Serves 6

1 oven-ready chicken (about 1.5 kg)
freshly ground black pepper
60 g butter
4 tbsp vegetable oil
salt
33 cl fruity white wine (for example,
Côtes-du-Rhône Cairenne blanc)
1 to 2 tbsp snipped fresh chives
baguettes for serving

For the crayfish sauce:
90 g butter
1 kg crayfish, plunged briefly into
boiling water by the fishmonger
4 cl brandy
4 shallots
4 garlic cloves
1 carrot
400 g tomatoes
½ litre fruity white wine
20 cl double cream

Preparation time: 1¼ hours

3,800 kJ/900 calories per portion

1 Wash the chicken and pat it dry. Divide into six joints and season with pepper. Preheat the oven to 150°C (300°F or Mark 2). Heat two frying pans, with 30 g butter and 2 tbsp oil in each, and fry the joints over medium heat for 5 to 8 minutes, until golden-brown, turning frequently. Season with salt and transfer to a large casserole or stockpot. Pour off the fat from the frying pan. Deglaze the pan with the wine, then pour it over the chicken.

2 Cover and cook in the centre of the oven for 40 to 45 minutes. Meanwhile, using one or two large frying pans with 30 g butter in each, fry the crayfish until bright red. Pour the brandy into a ladle. Hold the ladle over the rim or base of the pan to warm it, then pour the brandy over the crayfish, ignite it and flambé the shellfish *(above)*.

3 Reserve six crayfish for garnishing and wrap in foil. Twist off the pincers, heads and tails from the remainder.

Cut the pincers and shells with a knife or kitchen scissors and scrape out the meat *(bottom, left)*.

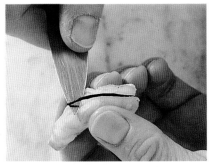

4 Cut the tail flesh with a knife and pull out the dark, vein-like intestine *(above)*. Reserve the meat and shells.

5 Peel and finely chop the shallots and garlic. Grate the carrot. Plunge the tomatoes into boiling water, then remove the skins and seeds. Chop roughly. Heat 30 g butter in a frying pan and fry the shallots and garlic over low heat. Add the carrot, tomatoes, white wine and crayfish shells. Cook, uncovered, over low heat for about 5 minutes, until most of the liquid has evaporated. Press it through a sieve, pressing out as much liquid as possible. Return it to the pan, add the cream and boil until reduced to about 12.5 cl. Season with salt and pepper.

6 Pour the pan juices from the chicken into a frying pan. Turn off the oven and keep the chicken and foil-wrapped crayfish warm in the oven. Reduce the pan juices to about 12.5 cl over high heat. Add to the sauce, season and add the crayfish meat. Return the sauce to the boil. Transfer the chicken to a warmed dish, pour over the sauce and garnish with the reserved crayfish and chives. Serve with baguettes.

Poulet au vinaigre

Easy • Lyonnais   **Chicken with creamy vinegar sauce**   *Serves 4*

**1 oven-ready chicken (preferably a
Bresse or corn-fed chicken,
about 1.6 kg)
25 to 50 g butter for frying
4 tbsp vegetable oil
salt • freshly ground white pepper
about ¼ litre white wine vinegar
25 to 50 g butter, straight from the
refrigerator, or 25 cl double
cream, to bind the sauce
4 thick slices brown rye bread
4 sprigs fresh tarragon (optional)**

**Preparation time: 30 minutes
(plus 40 to 50 minutes´ cooking
time)**

3,000 kJ/710 calories per portion

1 Wash the chicken, pat dry and divide into four portions. Heat the butter for frying and the oil in one or two large frying pans. Fry the chicken joints over medium heat for 8 to 10 minutes, until crisp and brown all round, turning frequently. Remove from the pan or pans and season with salt and pepper. Drain off the fat, deglaze the pan(s) with the vinegar, then reduce over high heat to about 12.5 cl. Lay the chicken, skin side upwards, in the stock in one frying pan. Cover and cook over low heat for 40 to 50 minutes.

2 Remove the chicken and keep warm. Stir the chilled butter into the sauce to bind it, or reduce the stock to 2 tbsp,

then add the cream, and reduce the sauce to about 12.5 cl. Adjust the seasoning, if necessary. Return the chicken joints to the sauce and warm through for 5 to 10 minutes.

3 Meanwhile, toast the bread on both sides. Place each slice of toast on a warmed plate with a chicken joint on top. Pour the sauce over the chicken. Garnish with tarragon sprigs or leaves, if wished, and serve immediately.

Wine: A full-flavoured red wine, such as Beaujolais-Villages, is excellent with *poulet au vinaigre.*

Poulet de Bresse à la crème

Easy • Bresse **Bresse chicken in cream sauce** *Serves 6*

1 oven-ready chicken (preferably a
Bresse or corn-fed chicken,
about 1.8 kg)
1 medium-sized onion
1 garlic clove • 5 cloves
150 g butter
salt • freshly ground white pepper
1 tbsp flour
¼ litre white wine
1 bouquet garni
25 cl double cream
juice of ½ lemon • 2 or 3 egg yolks
halved lemon slices for garnish

**Preparation time: 40 minutes
(plus 40 to 50 minutes' cooking
time)**

3,000 kJ/710 calories per portion

1 Preheat the oven to 180°C (350°F or Mark 4). Wash the chicken, pat dry and divide it into six joints. Peel the onion and garlic. Spike the onion with the cloves.

2 Heat the butter in one or two large frying pans. Fry the chicken joints for 8 to 12 minutes over medium heat, until lightly browned all over. Season with salt and pepper, and dust with flour. Remove from the pan. Save the fat for use in another dish.

3 Arrange the chicken in an ovenproof casserole. Add the wine, spiked onion, garlic and bouquet garni. Cover the casserole and cook in the centre of the oven for 40 to 50 minutes.

4 Strain the cooking juices through a sieve. Turn off the oven and leave the chicken in the casserole in the cooling oven. Transfer the strained cooking juices to a frying pan and reduce over high heat to about 2 tbsp. Stir in the cream and cook over medium heat for 2 to 3 minutes to make a smooth sauce. Season with the lemon juice, salt and pepper. Whisk the egg yolks with about 2 tbsp of the sauce. Return the egg yolk mixture to the hot, but not boiling, sauce and beat until creamy. Pour the sauce over the chicken. Leave to stand for 10 minutes. Garnish with lemon slices and serve with baguette.

Wine: Serve with a light white wine, such as Roussette du Bugey.

Poularde demi-deuil

Chicken poached with truffles

Serves 6

1 oven-ready chicken (about 1.5 kg)
2 black truffles (about 15 g each)
1 tbsp vegetable oil
freshly ground white pepper
salt
150 g chicken livers
200 g chicken breast fillets
15 g butter
1 egg white
22 cl double cream
2 leeks
3 litres chicken stock (see Note,
page 38)
4 small courgettes
12 small carrots
12 small white turnips
2 egg yolks

*Preparation time: 2 hours
(plus 24 hours' chilling time,
1½ hours for making the stock, if
necessary, and 2 hours' standing
time at room temperature)*

2,300 kJ/550 calories per portion

1 Wash the chicken and pat dry. Scrub and wash the truffles and pat dry. Cut one of the truffles into eight slices. Starting at the neck cavity of the chicken, insert two truffle slices at a time between the skin and the meat on each side of the breast, and on each thigh *(above)*. Season the chicken inside and out with pepper, then chill in the refrigerator for about 24 hours.

2 About 2 hours before you want to cook the chicken, remove it from the refrigerator and sprinkle it inside and out with salt.

3 Wash the chicken livers and chicken breast fillets, and pat them dry. Finely dice the livers. Heat the butter in a frying pan. Fry the livers for 10 to 15 seconds. Season with salt and pepper and leave to cool. Finely chop the second truffle and reserve ½ tsp of it for the sauce. Mince the breast fillets in a food processor, then mix with the diced livers, the rest of the chopped truffle, the egg white and 1 tbsp of the cream. Season with salt and pepper, and stuff the chicken with the mixture. Secure the body cavity with wooden toothpicks, or sew with kitchen twine.

4 Thoroughly wash the leeks. Cut each of them into three large chunks, using only the white parts. Bring the leeks to the boil in a large saucepan with the chicken stock. Add the chicken. Cover the saucepan and simmer in the stock over low heat for about 1¼ hours.

5 Meanwhile, wash the courgettes, carrots and turnips. Peel the carrots and turnips, leaving about 1 cm of stalk on each vegetable. Cut each of the courgettes diagonally into six oval pieces *(above)*. Take ¼ litre stock from the pan and boil each type of vegetable separately over high heat for 5 to 10 minutes. Drain and keep warm.

6 Transfer ½ litre of the stock to a second pan and reduce, uncovered, to about 12.5 cl over high heat. Mix the egg yolks and the rest of the cream with 12.5 cl of the hot stock. Pour the mixture into the reduced stock, then simmer over low heat to bind the sauce. Do not allow to boil, otherwise it may curdle.

7 Arrange the chicken on a warmed serving dish, surrounded by the hot vegetables. Sprinkle chopped truffle over the sauce. Serve the chicken at once, accompanied by the sauce.

Wine: Add the finishing touch to this festive chicken dish with an excellent red wine, such as Côte Rôtie from the Rhône Valley in eastern France.

VEGETABLES

I n France, vegetables are served not only as side dishes to main courses, they also make simple, nourishing meals in themselves. As with meat, vegetables are often cooked with mineral water or wine. Likewise, the same type of wine used in cooking is then drunk with the meal.

Cabbage is particularly popular. It is prepared in a variety of ways, from savoy cabbage simply fried with dripping or bacon, to sophisticated concoctions involving white wine, crème fraîche and a garnish of fried apples, prunes and chestnuts (recipe variation, page 107). In Alsace, sauerkraut made from white cabbage is a great favourite. Here, Riesling is used for cooking, whereas champagne is preferred in the Champagne region.

Green Puy lentils are a speciality of the Auvergne. Small and full-flavoured, they are served with game, pork and sausages, and as a creamy purée with poultry and lamb. Other popular purées are chestnut (recipe, page 104) to accompany game, and fragrant celeriac purée (recipe variation, page 108), which is served with fish and game dishes.

The potato dishes of eastern France are usually sufficiently satisfying to form a substantial part of the main meal. Depending on the region, potatoes are served boiled or fried, in the form of soufflés or creamed, sometimes with cheese added (recipes, pages 108-111).

Purée de châtaignes

Chestnut purée

1 kg chestnuts
1 stick celery
1 litre beef stock (see Note,
page 53)
freshly ground white pepper
sugar
30 g butter or crème fraîche
fresh chervil leaves for garnish

Preparation time: 1¼ hours
(plus 40 minutes' cooking time
and 1½ hours for making the
stock, if necessary)

1,200 kJ/290 calories per portion
(if serving 8)

1 Preheat the oven to 180°C (350°F or Mark 4). Make cross-shaped incisions in the tops of the chestnuts. Arrange them on a baking sheet and pour over 12.5 cl water. Roast the chestnuts in the centre of the oven for 10 minutes, or until they burst wide open. Allow to cool a little, then remove the shells and thin brown skin with a sharp knife. Cut in half. Discard any damaged ones.

2 Wash and coarsely chop the celery. Put the chestnuts and celery in a pan with the stock, cover and simmer over low heat for about 40 minutes, until the chestnuts are tender. Discard the celery. Rub the chestnuts through a coarse sieve. Add enough cooking liquid to make a smooth purée. Season with pepper and a little sugar. Using a

hand whisk, beat the butter or crème fraîche into the purée. Keep warm in a bain-marie until ready to serve. If it is made in advance, the purée can also be reheated in a bain-marie.

3 Transfer the purée to a bowl, or use an icing bag with a star-shaped nozzle to pipe it around the edge of a serving dish or individual plates. Serve the chestnut purée with game or poultry, garnished with chervil, if liked.

Note: For a more subtle flavour, boil the chestnuts in 1 litre milk instead of the stock, and season with salt, pepper and a little grated nutmeg.

Sweet chestnuts

In Limousin, chestnut trees have flourished for thousands of years. Chestnuts were an important staple food in rural France, right up to the end of the nineteenth century. Indeed, the sweet chestnut tree is still known as the bread tree, because chestnuts were commonly pounded into flour and used for bread making.

At the beginning of the eighteenth century, 40 per cent of Limousin's woodlands were given over to chestnut trees, but today only a few chestnut woods remain. About 100 tons of sweet chestnuts are harvested annually, but these are only enough to satisfy the needs of the local area—chestnuts, naturally enough, feature prominently in Limousin cuisine. Consequently, France has to import more than

10,000 tons of chestnuts a year from countries such as Spain and Portugal.

Sweet chestnut trees bear their fruit in spiky shells, grouped in clusters of between two and five. *Marrons*, the cultivated version of the wild *châtaigne*, are large and fat and grow singly inside the shell. They have a more cloying texture than the smaller chestnuts, and arguably a less delicate flavour. The finest of them are used to create the

luxurious sweets, *marrons glacés*.

Chestnuts are remarkably versatile and equally delicious in sweet dishes, in savoury stuffings, or as accompaniments to game or veal. The city of Limoges stages a cookery competition every two years, where chefs prepare a vast array of dishes aimed at showing just how inventive they can be with the unassuming sweet chestnut.

Choucroute à l'Alsacienne

Alsace sauerkraut

Not difficult • Alsace

Serves 4 to 6

1 kg raw sauerkraut
2 to 3 onions • 1 apple
2 to 3 garlic cloves
60 g goose or pork fat, or lard
1 bay leaf • 5 juniper berries
3 cloves • 5 peppercorns
sugar (optional)
about 12.5 cl chicken stock (see
Note, page 38)
¼ litre dry white wine

Preparation time: 30 minutes
(plus 2 to 4 hours' cooking time and
1½ hours for making the stock
if necessary)

740 kJ/180 calories per portion
(if serving 6)

1 Wash the sauerkraut, squeeze out the excess moisture, and spread on a dish. Peel the onions. Peel and core the apple. Peel the garlic. Finely chop the onions, apple and garlic.

2 Melt the goose or pork fat or lard in a large fireproof casserole or heavy pan over high heat. Fry the chopped ingredients for about 5 minutes. Gradually add the spices, sauerkraut and a little sugar, if using. Stir thoroughly, then add the chicken stock and wine. Cover and cook over low heat for 2 to 4 hours. Serve hot.

Note: Sauerkraut can be reheated without any loss of flavour. It is good served with goose, sausages, fish or creamed potatoes *(see page 108)*.

Variation: Choucroute garnie à l'Alsacienne
(Alsace sauerkraut garnished with mixed meat and sausages)
For 8 to 10 people, you need 3 pork knuckles (about 900 g each), 1 kg lightly smoked pork loin, 500 g smoked and 500 g salted bacon, and a selection of sausages. Cook the meat with the sauerkraut for the last 1½ hours. Grill the sausages. Garnish the sauerkraut with the meat and sausages, and serve accompanied by boiled potatoes.

Chou braisé

Braised savoy cabbage

Easy • Auvergne

Serves 6 to 8

salt
1 savoy cabbage (about 1 kg)
60 g goose fat or 100 g rindless
streaky bacon
freshly ground black pepper
12.5 cl fruity white wine (for
example, Saint-Pourçain)
100 g crème fraîche

Preparation time: 45 minutes

670 kJ/160 calories per portion
(if serving 8)

1 Bring some salted water to the boil in a large saucepan. Trim the cabbage, discarding the outer leaves, stalk and the ribs of the larger leaves, then wash. Turn off the heat under the pan and leave the cabbage to soak in the hot water for about 10 minutes, then plunge it into ice-cold water. Drain through a colander, then shred it.

2 Melt the goose fat in the pan over high heat (or fry the bacon, if using) and stir-fry the cabbage over high heat for about 5 minutes, until golden. Season with salt and pepper. Add the wine and crème fraîche, and simmer over low heat for about 20 minutes, until tender. Adjust the seasoning, if necessary, and serve at once.

Variation: Chou braisé aux pommes, aux pruneaux et aux châtaignes
(Braised savoy cabbage with apples, prunes and chestnuts)
This is the ideal accompaniment to roast turkey *(see page 92)*. Prepare the cabbage as described in the recipe. Soak 24 prunes in ½ litre hot black tea for about 30 minutes, then stone them. Cook 24 chestnuts *(see page 104)*. Peel 3 cooking apples, cut into eighths and remove the cores. Fry the apple wedges in a frying pan with 30 to 60 g butter for about 7 minutes. Add the prunes and chestnuts, and cook for a further 3 minutes, until the apple wedges are golden-brown. Arrange the cabbage and the rest of the ingredients on a warmed serving dish.

Purée de pommes de terre

Creamed potatoes

Simple · Many regions

Serves 4

4 floury potatoes (about 500 g)
salt
about 12.5 cl milk
freshly grated nutmeg
100 g butter, straight from the refrigerator (see Note)
freshly ground white pepper

Preparation time: 55 minutes

1,300 kJ/310 calories per portion

1 Wash and peel the potatoes, and cut into chunks. Place in a saucepan with enough salted water to cover. Boil over medium heat for 20 to 25 minutes.

2 Drain off the hot water and leave the potatoes in the pan over low heat until they stop steaming. Rub the potatoes through a sieve—do not use a food processor—into the pan. Place the pan on a hotplate to keep warm.

3 In another pan, bring the milk to the boil with a little grated nutmeg. Slice the ice-cold butter thinly. Beat it into the potatoes, using a wooden spoon.

4 Carefully stir in the hot milk a little at a time, to make a thick, creamy purée that is firm enough for you to make grooves in it with the wooden spoon. Season with pepper and serve.

Wine: Chablis, a dry white Burgundy, is perfect with creamed potatoes.

Note: The colder the butter, the more delicate the flavour of the purée will be. Creamed potatoes can be served with vegetables, mushrooms, egg dishes, fish, poultry, meat and offal. However, this version is so delicious, it can be eaten on its own.

Variation: Purée de céleri
(Celeriac purée)
Peel and wash 1 kg celeriac and cut into chunks. Place in a pan with 1 bay leaf and enough salted water to cover. Boil for 20 to 25 minutes, drain and discard the bay leaf. Rub the celeriac through a sieve. Whisk in 2 tbsp warmed crème fraîche, then beat 50 g ice-cold butter into the purée. Season with salt and pepper.

Aligot

Creamed potatoes with cheese

More complicated · Auvergne

Serves 4 to 6

800 g floury potatoes
salt
400 g Cantal or Caerphilly cheese
1 garlic clove
freshly ground white pepper
1 to 2 tbsp crème fraîche (optional)

Preparation time: 55 minutes

1,500 kJ/360 calories per portion (if serving 6)

1 Wash and peel the potatoes and cut into chunks. Place in a saucepan with enough salted water to cover. Boil over medium heat for 20 to 25 minutes. Thinly slice the cheese. Peel and halve the garlic and chop finely. Drain off the potato water and leave the potatoes in the pan over low heat until they stop steaming, then rub through a sieve—do not use a food processor. Stir in the garlic and return them to the pan.

2 Place the potatoes on a hotplate to keep warm. Season with pepper. Using a wooden spoon, stir the sliced cheese quickly and vigorously into the potato purée. Stir for 2 to 3 minutes, until the cheese has melted. Stir in the crème fraîche, if using, and serve.

Note: The French use the soft white unfermented Cantal cheese *Tomme de laguiole fraîche* for this dish. In its home region of the Auvergne, as cooks work the cheese into the potatoes with a wooden spoon they lift the mixture, stretching it like a wide elastic band up to a metre long without splitting it.
Aligot is good with sausages, or with a green salad, dressed with walnut oil.

Soufflé de pommes de terre

Easy • Savoy   **Potato and cheese soufflé**   *Serves 4*

500 g floury potatoes
salt
about 50 g butter
1 tbsp crème fraîche
3 egg yolks
100 g grated Beaufort or Gruyère cheese
freshly ground white pepper
freshly grated nutmeg
3 egg whites, at room temperature
2 tbsp finely chopped fresh parsley (optional)

Preparation time: 30 minutes (plus 20 to 30 minutes' cooking time)

1,600 kJ/380 calories per portion

1 Wash the potatoes, then place about 300 g of them, unpeeled, in a saucepan with enough salted water to cover. Boil for 20 to 25 minutes, then drain off the water and leave the potatoes to stand until they stop steaming. Preheat the oven to 250°C (450°F or Mark 8). Peel and very thinly slice the rest of the potatoes. Soak the slices in cold water for 1 to 2 minutes, then dry thoroughly with paper towels.

2 Melt about 25 g of the butter in a small pan over low heat, then coat the potato slices, one at a time, in the butter and lay them on a baking sheet. Cook on the top shelf of the oven for 2 to 3 minutes, turn them over and cook for a further 2 to 3 minutes, until golden-brown. Season the slices with salt. Reduce the oven temperature to 180°C (350°F or Mark 4).

3 Grease four 8 cm ramekins with the rest of the butter, and line with the crispy potatoes, arranged in a circle.

4 Peel the boiled potatoes and rub them through a sieve into a bowl. Stir in the crème fraîche, egg yolks and cheese. Season with pepper, nutmeg and, if necessary, salt. Whisk the egg whites with a pinch of salt until stiff. Using a spatula, fold the whites carefully into the creamed potatoes. Stir in the parsley, if using. Transfer to the ramekins and bake in the centre of the oven for 20 to 30 minutes, until golden-brown. Do not open the oven door while the soufflés are cooking, otherwise they will collapse.

5 Turn out the soufflés on to warmed plates. Serve as an accompaniment to mushrooms, fish or meat.

Pommes de terre lyonnaise

Sauté potatoes with onions   *Serves 4*

4 garlic cloves
about 125 g shallots or onions
500 g waxy potatoes
about 45 g butter
salt
freshly ground pepper
sprigs fresh flat-leaf parsley

Preparation time: 35 minutes

1,000 kJ/240 calories per portion

1 Peel the garlic and chop finely. Peel the shallots and cut into not-too-thin rings. Wash and peel the potatoes, then pat dry on paper towels and cut into slices about 5 mm thick.

2 Heat 15 g of the butter in a large frying pan and fry the shallot rings over medium heat for about 5 minutes, until golden-brown. Remove from the pan and reserve.

3 Add another 15 g of the butter to the pan and fry the potatoes in batches over high heat for 2 to 3 minutes, until golden-brown on both sides. Set aside while cooking the remainder. Add more butter with each batch of potatoes.

4 Return all the potatoes and shallots to the pan. Sprinkle with the chopped garlic. Season with salt and pepper. Fry over low heat for 5 to 8 minutes, until tender, turning the potato slices frequently. Wash the parsley, shake dry and chop finely.

5 Sprinkle the fried potatoes with the parsley and serve immediately, with dishes such as *cervelle de canut (see page 114)*.

Wine: In Lyon, this recipe would be served with a lightly chilled (14° to 16°C) red Beaujolais-Villages wine.

CHEESE

In France, cheese is served before the dessert, with wine—often with the same wine as the main course. Traditionally, you should offer only one type of cheese, one that harmonizes with the rest of the meal. Care should be taken to choose a wine that will not be overpowered by the aggressive flavour of the cheese, and ideally it should be from the same region. Here are some guidelines.

Cream cheese goes best with a dry rosé or white wine (for example, Saint-Pourçain). A fruity red *vin de pays*, such as Saint-Marcellin, suits cheeses with a white or bluish crust. Full-bodied reds are good with cheeses with rust-coloured rind, such as *Époisses*, but a spicy, aromatic Gewürztraminer from Alsace makes a pleasant accompaniment to *Munster*.

Blue-vein cheeses go well with red or fortified white wines. Hard cheeses (made with pressed curd), like Saint-Nectaire, can be enjoyed with dry or medium-dry white, rosé or red wine, but mature Cantal is worthy of a *cru*. With hard cheeses such as Comté, the best wine choices are white or dry rosé, while *vin jaune* is good with Beaufort cheese. Goat's milk cheeses are best served with local *vins de pays*, white, red or rosé.

Fresh fruit is also delicious served with cheese: grapes with goat cheese, apples with cheeses such as Comté, and pears with blue cheese.

Cervelle de canut

Simple • Lyonnais **Curd cheese with herbs** *Serves 4*

250 g curd cheese (40 per cent fat)
1 shallot
1 garlic clove
30 g mixed fresh herbs (tarragon,
chervil, parsley, chives)
1 tbsp dry white wine (for example,
Condrieu) or 1 tsp tarragon vinegar
1 tbsp virgin olive oil
100 g crème fraîche
salt
freshly ground black pepper

Preparation time: 35 minutes
(plus 12 to 24 hours' draining time
and 30 minutes' chilling time)

940 kJ/220 calories per portion

1 Place the curd cheese in a sieve and leave to drain for 12 to 24 hours. Peel and finely chop the shallot and garlic. Wash the herbs, shake and pat dry, then chop finely. Reserve 1 tbsp of the chopped herbs for garnishing.

2 Transfer the curd cheese to a bowl and beat vigorously with a hand whisk. Beat in the white wine or tarragon vinegar (both can be added, if wished) and olive oil. Add the crème fraîche, herbs, shallot and garlic. Beat thoroughly. Season with salt and pepper. Cover and leave to stand in the refrigerator for at least 30 minutes.

3 Just before serving, sprinkle the cheese with the reserved herbs. Serve with warm, crusty rye or nut bread.

Wine: Condrieu, a young fresh white wine from the Rhône Valley, is good with *cervelle de canut*. Red wine drinkers may prefer a slightly chilled Beaujolais-Villages.

Note: Although *cervelle* means "brain", the recipe *cervelle de canut*, sometimes called *cervelle des canuts*, has nothing to do with offal. It was a daily treat for *canuts* (silk weavers), who were so poor that they could only afford to eat meat on high days and holidays. The dish was often known as *claqueret*, because the curd cheese had to be beaten vigorously (*claquer* meaning to beat). In Lyon, *cervelle de canut* is eaten with ham and potatoes boiled in their skins. To serve this way, double the quantities given here.

Cream

In our grandparents' day, cream-making was simple but slow. Milk was left to stand in a cool place for twenty-four hours or so, and when the cream rose to the top it was skimmed from the surface. Today, a centrifuge is used to spin the milk and separate off the cream. Double cream is the richest with a 48 per cent fat content, whipping has 35 per cent, single has 18 per cent and half cream 12 per cent.

Crème fraîche, which is widely used in French cooking for both sweet and savoury dishes, is a lightly cultured cream with a distinctive, slightly sharp taste. The usual fat content is 35 per cent, but there is also low calorie crème fraîche with a fat content of 12 to 15 per cent. *Crème fraîche épaisse*, a thick, firm crème fraîche available in France, undergoes a longer maturing process. *Crème liquide*, or *crème fleurette*, is a semi-liquid single cream.

The different creams all have their roles to play in French cuisine. Double and single cream and *crème fraîche épaisse* can be added to pan juices and reduced to a smooth, thick sauce. *Crème fraîche* is stirred into sauces and stocks at the end of the cooking time; the reduced calorie version should be added just before serving, and not allowed to boil.

Fromage aux raisins

Cheese with raisins

Prepare in advance • Burgundy

Serves 8

50 to 100 g raisins or sultanas
¼ litre ratafia or marc (see
Glossary) • 500 g soft cheese

Preparation time: 25 minutes
(plus 24 hours' soaking time
and 24 hours' chilling time)

1,000 kJ/240 calories per portion

1 Wash the raisins or sultanas until the water runs clear. Pat dry and leave to soak in the ratafia for 24 hours.

2 Using a wooden spoon, thoroughly mix the cheese and soaked raisins, then transfer the cheese mixture to a glass or stoneware jar and store in the refrigerator for 24 hours. (The mixture can be kept in the refrigerator until the "use by" date indicated on the cheese packaging, if wished.)

3 Serve the cheese with raisins at room temperature, accompanied by *pain viennois* (a soft, plump baguette) or any other freshly made French white bread cut into chunks.

Crème de fromage aux noix

Cheese and walnut cream

Simple • Auvergne

Serves 4

250 g mild blue cheese
75 g shelled walnuts
200 g crème fraîche
freshly ground white pepper

Preparation time: 25 minutes
(plus at least 3 hours' chilling time)

2,200 kJ/520 calories per portion

1 Cut off the cheese rind, then mash the cheese with a fork. Reserve a few walnuts and finely chop the rest.

2 Whisk the crème fraîche until stiff, taking care as it quickly becomes buttery if overbeaten. Fold the crème fraîche into the cheese with a spatula. Season with pepper. Stir the chopped walnuts into the cheese. Transfer the mixture to a stoneware pot, or four small ramekins, if preferred. Chill in the refrigerator for at least 3 hours.

3 Serve the cheese and walnut cream at room temperature, garnished with the reserved walnuts, accompanied by thin slices of toast.

Salade au Bresse bleu

Salad with blue cheese dressing

Quick • Bresse

Serves 4

1 round or cos lettuce
15 g fresh chives
200 g Bresse bleu or other blue
cow's milk cheese
200 to 250 g crème fraîche
salt • freshly ground black pepper
cayenne pepper

Preparation time: 30 minutes

1,800 kJ/430 calories per portion

1 Wash the round or cos lettuce and the chives. Dry the lettuce leaves in a salad spinner. Shake the chives dry and snip into small pieces.

2 Mash the blue cheese with a fork and mix it thoroughly with the crème fraîche. Rub the mixture through a sieve for a smoother finish, if liked. Season to taste with salt, pepper and a little cayenne pepper.

3 Arrange the lettuce leaves on four individual plates and spoon the cheese into the centre. Sprinkle chives over the top. Serve with slices of baguette or other crusty white bread.

Wine: Unlike most salad dressings, this one contains no vinegar or lemon juice, so you can serve the salad with a Côte Rôtie, a delicate red wine from the Rhône vineyards.

Pétafine

Cheese pâté

Prepare in advance • Dauphiné

Serves 10

500 g cream cheese (see Note)
3 garlic cloves • 100 g crème fraîche
freshly ground black pepper
2 to 3 tbsp eau-de-vie or marc

Preparation time: 15 minutes
(plus 3 days' chilling time)

960 kJ/230 calories per portion

1 Crumble the cheese into a bowl. Peel the garlic and chop finely. Add to the cheese and stir thoroughly with a fork. Stir in the crème fraîche. Season with pepper and eau-de-vie.

2 Transfer the mixture to a stoneware or glass jar. Cover and leave in the refrigerator for 3 days. (The cheese pâté will keep until the "use by" date shown on the crème fraîche tub.) Serve at room temperature, with slices of coarse rye bread or baguettes.

Note: For best results, use half cow's milk cheese and half goat's milk cheese with a fat content of about 40 per cent.

Fromage fort

Fermented cheese

Prepare in advance • Burgundy

Serves 10

250 g Comté or Gruyère cheese
2 dried goat's cheeses (60 g each
—see Note)
100 g fresh butter • 1 tbsp olive oil
12.5 cl dry white wine • 3 tbsp marc
freshly ground black pepper

Preparation time: 20 minutes
(plus at least 3 days' chilling time)

1,100 kJ/260 calories per portion

1 Remove the cheese rind and grate the cheese very finely. In a bowl, mix the butter and oil together with a fork. Stir just enough wine into the cheese to create a creamy texture. Season to taste with the marc and pepper.

2 Transfer the cheese mixture to a glass or stoneware jar. Cover the jar and leave to stand in the refrigerator for at least 3 days before using.

3 Serve at room temperature with crusty bread or spread the cheese on slices of bread and cook under the grill for 3 to 4 minutes.

Note: This recipe uses dried goat's cheese, readily available in France. You can dry fresh goat's cheese (the type with a soft rind, not the sort in plastic tubs); at room temperature it takes four to eight weeks.

Cancoillotte

Jura soft cheese

Simple • Franche-Comté

Serves 6

1 to 2 garlic cloves
200 g each 3 piquant cheeses (for
example, Époisses, Langres and
Maroilles)
30 g softened butter
12.5 cl tangy white wine

Preparation time: 20 minutes

390 kJ/93 calories per portion

1 Peel the garlic and chop finely. Place the cheeses in a saucepan with the butter and melt over very low heat, whisking constantly. Bring to the boil. Add just enough wine to make a thick paste. Add the garlic.

2 Serve the cheese hot with potatoes boiled in their skins, or cold as a tasty spread on slices of bread or toast.

Variation: In France, this is made with *metton* (curdled skimmed milk). Heat about 10 cl milk. In a jar about 15 cm in diameter mix the *metton* with 30 g softened butter and salt. Cover with the milk and leave to stand for about 1½ hours. Transfer the mixture to a pan and melt over very low heat, whisking. Add just enough wine to create a thick paste. Add the garlic.

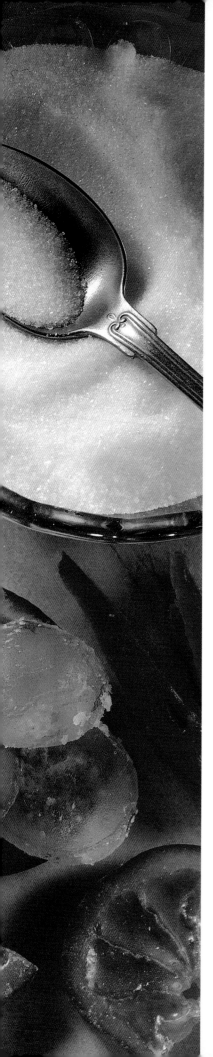

DESSERTS

A sked to choose between cheese or a dessert, most French people will opt for cheese. The French have a passion for cheese, but as they are also very partial to sweet things, they would ideally like to be offered both.

In rural eastern France and the Massif Central, desserts are as down-to-earth as the rest of the cuisine. Many are made with the staple ingredients of eggs and cream. Flat cakes, called *galettes*, may be topped with crème fraîche, custard, curd cheese or fruit. As soon as the oven is no longer needed for the main course, in go the cakes, making sure that they are ready in time for the end of the meal. *Galettes* taste best of all while still warm.

Summer desserts are lighter: ice cream or fruit in season, served on its own or with lightly sweetened, whipped crème fraîche.

If you have served red wine with the main course or cheese, you can safely offer the same wine with a cake containing red fruit. For a more festive touch, choose a champagne-style wine, or, on special occasions, real champagne.

Every French meal ends with *un p'tit noir* (espresso), and after dinner a *digestif.* Depending on the region, this may be *marc* or *eau-de-vie.*

Baba au kirsch

Takes time • Lorraine

Yeast cake with kirsch

Serves 6 to 8

For the batter:
20 g yeast
3 tbsp lukewarm milk
80 g butter • 250 g plain flour
30 g sugar
salt • 3 eggs
butter for greasing

For the syrup:
150 g sugar
6 to 8 tbsp kirsch, other fruit
brandy, or rum

To decorate:
6 to 8 tbsp apricot jam
candied fruits
50 cl ice-cold whipping cream
30 to 50 g icing sugar

Preparation time: 35 minutes
(plus 2 hours' proving time
and 35 minutes' cooking time)

2,600 kJ/620 calories per portion
(if serving 8)

1 Crumble the yeast and stir into the milk until smooth. Melt the butter in a saucepan. Using a hand whisk, beat 100 g of the flour, the yeast mixture, sugar, a little salt and one egg in a large bowl. Add the remaining eggs and the rest of the flour alternately, and mix thoroughly. Add the melted butter, then beat the mixture for about 5 minutes, until soft and smooth.

2 Cover the bowl with a clean cloth and leave the batter to rise in a warm place for about 1½ hours. Butter a 24 cm savarin or ring mould or 6 to 8 individual moulds.

3 Whisk the yeast batter for a further 5 minutes. Fill the mould or individual moulds (these should be only one-third full with the batter). Leave to prove for another 30 minutes. Preheat the oven to 200°C (400°F or Mark 6).

4 Bake the cake on the bottom shelf of the oven for 30 to 35 minutes, until it is crisp and brown, and a fine skewer inserted into it comes out clean.

5 Place the sugar for the syrup in a pan with ¼ litre water and boil over high heat until reduced to a syrup.

6 Turn out the cake on to a wire rack placed over a plate while still warm and ladle the hot syrup evenly over the top, allowing any excess to collect on the plate under the wire rack. Sprinkle immediately with the kirsch. Spoon the syrup from the plate over the cake.

7 Sieve the jam and spread it over the cake. Decorate with candied fruits.

8 Just before serving, whip the cream until stiff. Fold in the icing sugar and whip until stiff again. Transfer the cream to an icing bag fitted with a star nozzle. Pipe a mound of cream into the hollow centre of the cake and decorate with stars of cream, then pipe cream stars over the surface of the cake or around the edge of the serving plate. Decorate the cake with more candied fruits, if liked.

Drink: Kirsch goes well with *baba au kirsch*. With *baba au rhum* (rum baba), serve a sparkling Crémant d'Alsace, a white wine made in a similar way to champagne.

Variation: Kugelhopf

(Alsatian yeast cake)

Soak 75 g sultanas in 6 to 8 tbsp kirsch for at least 24 hours. Prepare the batter as described in the recipe, using double the quantities. Butter a fluted 1.5 litre *kugelhopf* mould and place a blanched almond in each groove of the mould. Stir the sultanas and kirsch into the batter just before transferring it to the mould. Leave the batter to rise in the mould until it reaches the rim. Bake on the bottom shelf of the oven at 200°C (400°F or Mark 6) for 30 to 35 minutes. Turn out of the mould and sprinkle with icing sugar when cold. Serve a perfumed wine, such as Gewürztraminer, or Crémant d'Alsace with this kugelhopf.

Note: There are several different versions of the story of how the baba was invented. One story concerns Polish King Stanislas Leszczinsky, father-in-law of King Louis XV. Kugelhopf was his favourite delicacy, but, on one occasion, finding the cake too dry, he poured some sweet Malaga wine over it. Since he was also a fan of the story "One Thousand and One Nights", he named his creation after the hero, Ali Baba—it was then shortened to baba. In time it became customary to soak baba in rum.

Sabayon au champagne

Frothy champagne dessert

Serves 6

5 very fresh egg yolks, at room temperature (see Note)
150 g caster sugar
¼ bottle champagne
6 pistachio nuts

Preparation time: 10 minutes

810 kJ/190 calories per portion

1 In a metal bowl or saucepan in a bain-marie, whisk the egg yolks and sugar with a hand whisk for 5 minutes, until frothy. When the mixture is pale and creamy, gradually whisk in the champagne. Continue whisking the mixture vigorously, preferably using a figure of eight movement, until the cream is frothy.

2 Serve immediately in six champagne glasses, decorated with pistachio nuts.

Note: Make sure you use only very fresh eggs from a reliable source. The very young, the elderly, pregnant women and anyone with problems with their immune system are advised not to eat raw or lightly cooked eggs because of the risk of salmonella.

Variation: Crème champenoise
(Champagne cream)
Grate the rind of an unwaxed lemon and 5 cubes of sugar. Dissolve the sugar in about ¼ litre champagne. Whisk 5 egg yolks with the champagne, as described left, until the mixture thickens. Remove the bowl from the bain-marie and continue to whisk until cool. Whisk the 5 egg whites and a little salt in a clean, grease-free bowl until they peak. Fold them into the cooled egg yolk mixture. Transfer to a bowl and chill for 2 to 3 hours. Serve chilled with sponge fingers.

Champagne

True champagne can only come from the Champagne region of northeast France. The world's most famous sparkling wine was created here at the end of the seventeenth century by Dom Pérignon, a Benedictine monk, who discovered how to capture the effervescence released as the local wine fermented by using strengthened bottles with corks tied down by string.

The ritual of making champagne by the traditional process is known as *méthode champenoise*. After the grape harvest has taken place at the end of September, the grapes are pressed and the juice from each vineyard is fermented separately.

The wines for each particular *cru* (a system of classes for champagne) are tasted and then made into a *cuvée*, or blend. In a year when the grapes are especially good and plentiful, a vintage is declared and a champagne is made from the grapes of that year alone.

The bubbles are created by inducing a second fermentation in the bottle. Stored in cool cellars cut deep into the chalk rock, with a constant level of humidity, the champagne is left to mature for at least one year, and ideally up to three years.

Œufs à la neige

"Snow eggs"

More complicated • Lyonnais

Serves 4 to 6

For the meringues:
4 very fresh eggs, at room
temperature (see Note)
salt
80 g caster sugar

For cooking the meringues:
½ vanilla pod
¾ litre milk
40 g caster sugar

For the custard:
40 g caster sugar

Preparation time: 50 minutes

1,200 kJ/290 calories per portion
(if serving 6)

1 Separate the eggs, reserving the yokes for the custard (Step 3). In a grease-free bowl, whisk the egg whites with a little salt until they stand in stiff peaks. Drizzle the 80 g caster sugar into the stiff egg whites and continue to whisk for a further 5 minutes. Draw a line through the beaten egg whites with a knife. If the line remains visible, they are stiff enough *(above)*.

2 Cut the vanilla pod open. Bring the milk, sugar and vanilla pod to the boil in a high-sided saucepan over medium heat. Briefly remove the pan from the heat. Turn down the heat and return the saucepan to the hob, so that the milk simmers. Using two wet tablespoons, shape the egg whites into three "snowballs" per portion *(above)*. Lower the meringues, one at a time, into the simmering milk and cook for no more than 10 seconds on each side. Remove the meringues with a slotted spoon and drain on paper towels.

3 To make the custard, whisk the egg yolks and the 40 g sugar in the top of a double boiler or a heatproof bowl set over a pan of simmering water until frothy. Gradually add ½ litre of the hot milk, stirring constantly. Continue to stir the custard until it is thick enough to coat the back of a spoon *(above)*.

4 Whisk the custard over a bain-marie of cold water, using a hand whisk. When cool, pour it into a glass bowl or individual dessert bowls. Carefully spoon the "snowballs" on top of the cooled custard.

Note: Make sure you use only very fresh eggs from a reliable source. The very young, the elderly, pregnant women and anyone with problems with their immune system are advised not to eat raw or very lightly cooked eggs because of the risk of salmonella.

It is best to eat *œufs à la neige* as soon as possible as they lose their fragrance after 2 to 3 hours.

Gâteau au fromage blanc

Cheesecake with fruit sauce

Plan in advance • Bresse
Serves 4 to 6

For the cake:
500 g curd cheese (40 per cent fat)
butter for greasing
125 g sugar
50 g flour
grated rind of 1 unwaxed lemon
3 very fresh egg whites
salt
fresh mint leaves for garnish

For the fruit sauce:
300 g fresh strawberries or
raspberries • 2 tbsp sugar
1 tbsp kirsch or raspberry brandy

Preparation time: 35 minutes
(plus 4 hours' draining time and
35 to 40 minutes' baking time)

1,300 kJ/310 calories per portion
(if serving 6)

1 Place the curd cheese in a sieve and leave to drain for about 4 hours, then wrap in paper towels until dry.

2 Preheat the oven to 180°C (350°F or Mark 4). Butter a 26 cm round gratin dish or four to six small gratin dishes.

3 Using a hand whisk, stir the sugar, then the flour and finally the grated lemon rind into the cheese. Beat the egg whites with a little salt until stiff. Using a spatula, carefully fold the egg whites into the cheese mixture. Spoon the mixture into the gratin dishes.

4 Pour hot water into a roasting pan to a depth of about two fingers. Place the dishes in the pan. Bake in the centre of the oven for 35 to 40 minutes, until the cake has risen slightly. Leave to cool in the oven with the door open.

5 Sort and wash the fruit and pat dry. Reserve 4 to 6 well-shaped berries for decoration. Purée the rest of the fruit and sugar in a blender. Stir in the kirsch or raspberry brandy.

6 Divide the fruit sauce between four to six plates. The cake can be served warm or at room temperature. Cut into slices, or turn out of individual dishes, and place on top of the fruit sauce. Decorate with the mint leaves and the reserved berries cut in half, and serve at once.

Wine: Serve this fruit gâteau with a Montagnieu, a champagne-type wine from the Bugey region.

Matefaim

Not difficult • Franche-Comté

Pancakes with fruit filling

Serves 4

100 g butter, at room temperature
1 egg • 2 egg yolks
3 tbsp sugar • salt
125 g plain flour
20 cl milk • 1 tsp kirsch

For the fruit filling:
250 g each fresh raspberries and blackberries
40 to 80 g sugar (optional)

To finish:
fresh mint leaves for garnish
icing sugar for dusting

Preparation time: 40 minutes
(plus 2 hours' resting time)

1,900 kJ/450 calories per portion

1 Place 15 g of the butter, the egg, egg yolks, sugar and a little salt in a bowl and whisk until frothy. Add the flour and milk, and mix to a smooth pancake batter. Stir in the kirsch, then leave to rest at room temperature for at least 2 hours.

2 Wash and hull the fruit. Reserve half the fruit for the filling. Keeping the raspberries and blackberries separate, purée them in a blender. Sweeten with a little sugar, if liked. Pour a pool of both types of sauce onto four large dessert plates.

3 Heat some of the remaining butter in a frying pan (use two, if preferred). Pour in enough batter to coat the base of the pan and cook over medium heat for 2 to 3 minutes on each side. Keep

the pancake warm. Repeat to make a total of eight pancakes, adding more butter for each pancake.

4 Top four pancakes with raspberries and four with blackberries, and fold over. Arrange one raspberry and one blackberry pancake in each pool of sauce. Decorate with mint leaves and dust with icing sugar. Serve at once.

Variation: Any soft fruit in season—strawberries for example—may be used for the sauce and the pancake filling.

Note: The name of this dessert, *matefaim*, is a reminder that Franche-Comté was for many years occupied by Spanish troops. The old Spanish *mata fame* became first *matafam* and then *matefaim*. Today it is known as *matahambre*. The French version is *tue la faim* (literally: kill the hunger).

Flognarde aux poires

Simple • Auvergne **Pears in pancake batter** *Serves 6*

butter for greasing
2 eggs
50 g sugar
salt
3 tbsp flour
¼ litre milk
3 tbsp pear brandy (for example,
Poire Williams)
3 ripe pears
1 tbsp sugar mixed with 1 tsp
ground cinnamon for sprinkling

*Preparation time: 20 minutes
(plus 30 minutes' cooking time)*

720 kJ/170 calories per portion

1 Preheat the oven to 200°C (400°F or Mark 6). Butter a 28 cm round gratin dish. Whisk the eggs, sugar and a little salt in a bowl until frothy. Stir in the flour, milk and brandy alternately, a little at a time.

2 Wash and peel the pears, then cut in half and remove the cores. Arrange the pears, cut side downwards, in the dish and pour the batter over the top. Bake the pudding in the centre of the oven for about 30 minutes, until the batter rises and turns golden.

3 Remove from the oven and sprinkle the cinnamon sugar over the top. Serve at once, straight from the dish.

Variations:

Flognarde aux poires et aux noix
(Pears in nut batter)
Instead of flour, use 3 tbsp ground nuts of your choice. Use 4 to 5 tbsp cream instead of milk.

Clafoutis
(Cherries in pancake batter)
Prepare in the same way as *flognarde aux poires*, but replace the pears with 500 g small, unstoned, black cherries, and stir kirsch instead of brandy into the batter. Dust with icing sugar instead of cinnamon sugar.

Biscuit de Savoie aux poires

Make ahead • Savoy **Sponge cake with cinnamon pears** *Serves 4 to 6*

For the sponge:
butter for greasing
4 eggs, at room temperature
salt • 155 g caster sugar
grated rind of 1 unwaxed lemon
50 g potato flour • 50 g plain flour
2 tbsp flaked almonds
125 g whipping cream

For the filling:
4 ripe pears • 30 g butter
2 tbsp sugar • 5 tbsp white wine (for
example, Vin de Savoie)
1 cinnamon stick

Preparation time: 1¾ hours

*1,900 kJ/450 calories per portion
(if serving 6)*

1 Preheat the oven to 180°C (350°F or Mark 4). Butter a 24 cm round springform cake tin. Separate the eggs. Whisk the yolks in a bowl with a little salt and 125 g of the sugar, until creamy. Stir the grated lemon rind, potato flour and plain flour into the egg yolk mixture.

2 In a grease-free bowl, beat the egg whites with a little salt until stiff. Using a spatula, fold the beaten egg whites into the sponge mixture.

3 Pour the mixture into the greased cake tin. Sprinkle with 2 tbsp sugar and the flaked almonds. Bake on the bottom shelf of the oven for 35 to 45 minutes, until lightly browned.

4 Meanwhile, make the filling. Wash and peel the pears. Cut into eighths and remove the cores. Heat the butter and sugar in a large frying pan over high heat. Add the pears and shake the pan until all the pear wedges are caramelized. Stir in the white wine. Break the cinnamon stick into two or three pieces and add them to the pears. Cover the pan and simmer over low heat for 5 to 10 minutes. Discard the pieces of cinnamon stick.

5 Turn the sponge out of the tin while still warm. Slice in half horizontally. Arrange the cooked pears over the bottom half of the sponge, then cover with the other half. Cut into wedges and serve warm, with whipped cream.

Kouglhopf glace Williams

Pear parfait in a kugelhopf mould

Make ahead • Alsace

Serves 6 to 8

**6 pears (for example, William
—about 800 g)**
4 to 6 tbsp currants
**12.5 cl pear brandy (for example,
Poire Williams)**
1 to 2 tbsp flaked almonds
8 very fresh egg yolks (see Note)
400 g sugar
60 cl ice-cold whipping cream
cocoa powder for dusting

**Preparation time: 30 minutes
(plus 24 hours' soaking time
and 12 hours' freezing time)**

**2,500 kJ/600 calories per portion
(if serving 8)**

1 Wash and peel the pears. Cut into quarters and core them, then dice finely. Wash the currants and pat dry. Divide the brandy between two bowls and soak the diced pears and currants separately for about 24 hours.

2 Line a 1.5 litre metal kugelhopf mould with flaked almonds. Whisk the egg yolks and sugar until frothy. Purée the pears, with or without the brandy. Pat the currants dry. Stir the currants and the pear purée into the egg yolk mixture. Whip the cream in an ice-cold bowl until stiff and carefully fold it into the pear mixture, using a spatula. Pour the mixture into the mould and freeze for at least 12 hours.

3 Dip the mould briefly in hot water. Turn out the pear parfait. Dust with cocoa powder and serve immediately. Divide into portions at the table.

Note: Make sure you use only very fresh eggs from a reliable source. The very young, the elderly, pregnant women and anyone with problems with their immune system are advised not to eat raw or very lightly cooked eggs because of the risk of salmonella.

Variation: For a quicker version, stir the brandy-soaked pears and currants into about 1 kg vanilla ice cream, then transfer to the almond-lined mould and freeze for at least 4 hours.

Truffes

Chocolate truffles

*250 g plain chocolate (containing
more than 50 per cent cocoa)*
*2 very fresh egg yolks (see Note,
opposite)*
2 to 3 tbsp icing sugar
100 g very fresh butter
1 to 2 tbsp crème fraîche
1 tbsp rum (optional)
4 tbsp unsweetened cocoa powder

*Preparation time: 1 hour
(plus 7 hours' chilling time)*

320 kJ/76 calories per truffle

1 Break the chocolate into pieces and melt it in a heatproof bowl set over a pan of simmering water or the top of a double boiler. Meanwhile, beat the egg yolks in a bowl until frothy, using a hand whisk. Add the icing sugar and continue to whisk. Remove the melted chocolate from the heat. Dice the butter and stir it into the chocolate. Add the egg yolks, crème fraîche and rum, if using.

2 Stir the chocolate mixture with a wooden spoon until smooth. Pour on to a sheet of aluminium foil. Shape the chocolate into a rectangular block (like a flat pack of butter), measuring about 10 by 20 cm. Wrap it in foil and chill for at least 6 hours.

3 Sift 2 tbsp cocoa powder on to a work surface. Unwrap the chocolate

and lay it on top. Sprinkle with the rest of the cocoa powder. Using a knife, cut the block lengthwise into eight and crosswise into four. Roll the squares into small balls in the cocoa powder, until well coated. Arrange the truffles in paper petits fours cases and chill for at least 1 hour.

Note: Truffles will keep in a closed box in the refrigerator as long as the eggs remain completely fresh. The chocolate truffles taste best served at room temperature.

Variations: You can flavour truffles with orange liqueur, kirsch or a dash of strong espresso coffee, instead of rum. You can also coat them in icing sugar, if preferred.

Bugnes de Lyon
Lyonnais doughnuts

10 g fresh yeast
300 to 350 g plain flour
50 g sugar
salt
50 g butter, at room temperature
2 eggs
2 to 3 cl rum
grated rind of 1 unwaxed lemon
vegetable fat or oil for deep frying
icing sugar for dusting

Preparation time: 1¾ hours
(plus 2 hours' resting time and
24 hours' chilling time)

2,400 kJ/570 calories per portion
(if serving 8)

1 Crumble the yeast into a large bowl and dissolve in 2 to 3 tbsp lukewarm water. Using the pastry hook of a food processor, knead the flour, sugar, a little salt, the yeast, butter, eggs, rum and lemon rind to a smooth dough which comes away from the sides of the bowl. Shape the dough into a ball, sprinkle with a little flour, cover with a clean cloth and leave to rest for 1 to 2 hours. Knead the dough for 5 to 10 minutes, wrap in a cloth and chill in the refrigerator for 12 to 24 hours.

2 On a lightly floured work surface, roll out the dough to a thickness of about 5 mm. Using a small pastry wheel, cut the pastry into rectangular strips about 3 by 20 cm. Cut a 3 cm slit about a third of the way along each strip of pastry, then pull the other end of the strip through the slit to make a loop *(above)*.

3 Heat the fat or oil for frying in a heavy-based deep saucepan or a deep-fat fryer until very hot. When small bubbles rise from a wooden chopstick dipped in the hot fat, immediately turn the heat down to medium. Fry the doughnuts in batches of three to five in the hot fat for 2 to 3 minutes, until golden-brown. Drain the doughnuts on paper towels and dust with icing sugar while they are still warm.

Wine: A light red wine, such as a Beaujolais or Beaujolais-Villages, is usually served with these doughnuts.

Variation: Bugnes
(Mini-doughnuts)
To serve 8 to 10, mix 500 g plain flour, 20 g baking powder, 125 g sugar, a little salt, 250 g butter, 4 eggs and 2 cl rum (optional) to a smooth dough. Using a spoon, shape the dough into walnut-sized pieces. Fry in vegetable fat or oil as described above. Sprinkle with icing sugar. Mini-doughnuts will keep for one or two days.

Note: In the old days, *bugnes* were simple made with water, flour, yeast and rose water. This mixture made such light doughnuts, that it used to be said of any inhabitant of Lyon on his deathbed "He will float up to Heaven like a *bugne*."

Another story relates how, for centuries, *bugnes* were dull, almost tasteless cakes eaten during Lent. Fortunately, Lyon's confectioners came up with the idea of improving the thin dough, much to the delight of the clientele. The Archbishop wanted to excommunicate all the sinful doughnut-eaters, but this version of *bugnes* became so popular that he was obliged to be merciful or risk losing his whole congregation.

Bugnes have now become a well-loved pre-Easter treat, sold by every *patisserie* in Lyon, especially on Shrove Tuesday. Fried *bugnes* made with a yeast dough taste best when served immediately.

Gâteau grenoblois

Grenoble walnut sponge cake

butter for greasing
250 g shelled walnuts
100 g butter • 150 g caster sugar
3 egg yolks • 100 g plain flour
1 tsp baking powder
5 egg whites • 2 cl rum (optional)
icing sugar for dusting (optional)

For the cream filling:
¼ litre milk • ½ vanilla pod
2 egg yolks • 50 g sugar
25 g flour • 12.5 cl whipping cream
50 g icing sugar

Preparation time: 1¼ hours
(plus 45 to 60 minutes' baking time,
1 hour's cooling time and 12 hours'
chilling time)

2,000 kJ/480 calories per portion
(if serving 10)

1 Heat the oven to 175°C (350°F or Mark 4). Butter a 26 cm round springform cake tin. Reserve 8 to 10 walnut halves for decoration. Finely chop 100 g of the walnuts, and finely grind the rest. Line the tin with 1 tbsp of the ground walnuts. Cream the butter and sugar until fluffy. Stir in the egg yolks, chopped walnuts, flour and baking powder. Whisk the egg whites in a grease-free bowl until stiff. Using a spatula, carefully fold the egg whites into the cake mixture, then transfer it to the cake tin. Immediately place it in the centre of the oven and bake for 45 to 60 minutes. Turn the sponge out of the tin and leave to cool.

2 To make the filling, heat the milk and vanilla pod in a deep saucepan. Whisk the egg yolks in a bowl with the sugar and flour, until frothy. Slowly stir the milk into the egg mixture. Pour into the pan and whisk over very low heat for 3 to 5 minutes, until thick. Leave to cool for about 1 hour. Whip the cream with the icing sugar until stiff and fold carefully into the custard.

3 Cut the sponge horizontally into three slices. Sprinkle with rum, if using. Spread a quarter of the cream filling over the bottom slice. Lay the second slice on top, and spread with another quarter of the filling. Repeat this again with the third slice. Spread the rest of the cream round the side of the cake, and sprinkle with the remaining ground walnuts. Decorate with walnut halves and dust with icing sugar. Leave to chill in the refrigerator for at least 12 hours and serve cold.

Tarte au goumeau

Custard tart

For the shortcrust pastry:
100 g very cold butter
200 g plain flour • 60 g sugar • salt
5 tbsp milk • butter for greasing

For the custard:
2 eggs • 100 g sugar • salt
100 g crème fraîche • 12.5 cl milk
1 tbsp orange flower water

Preparation time: 25 minutes
(plus 30 minutes' resting time and
30 minutes' baking time)

1,500 kJ/360 calories per portion
(if serving 8)

1 Butter a 26 cm springform cake tin. To make the pastry, place the flour, sugar and a little salt in a bowl. Cut the cold butter into thin slices and rub it into the flour until the consistency resembles breadcrumbs. Stir in just enough milk to make a smooth dough. Transfer the dough to the tin, shaping a 2 cm-high border with your fingers. Leave to rest in the refrigerator for about 30 minutes.

2 Meanwhile preheat the oven to 200°C (400°F or Mark 6). Blind-bake the pastry in the centre of the oven for 5 to 10 minutes. While the pastry is cooking, mix the eggs, sugar, a little salt, crème fraîche, milk and orange flower water with a hand whisk. Pour the custard into the pastry shell and return to the oven to cook for about 30 minutes, until the custard has turned golden and doubled in volume.

Wine: Sparkling white wine, such as Crémant, is delicious served with warm custard tart.

Variation: If orange flower water is unavailable, or if you do not like the taste, stir the seeds from half a vanilla pod into the custard instead.

Suggested Menus

The following selection of menus will give you some idea of French eating habits. In rural areas, the whole family sits down to meals together, even on weekdays. Side dishes to accompany the menu suggestions below can be chosen from the vegetable chapter starting on page 103.

In France, the main course is followed by a green salad with a vinaigrette dressing—even when the meal has begun with a salad starter. Even weekday meals include a little piece of cheese before the dessert, and the meal ends with a small coffee, *un p'tit noir* (espresso).

Preparations for traditional Sunday and feast day meals begin the night before, at the latest. For picnics, all the families taking part share the task of preparing the food. Easter and Christmas are celebrated by large family reunions, while it is traditional to see in the New Year at a restaurant. Since the beginning of January marks the end of the hunting season, New Year's Day is the last opportunity to serve roast game.

The recipe quantities given for the three course meals are enough to satisfy even the most hearty eaters. However, since it is customary in France to remain at the meal table for hours on end, enjoying dishes lovingly prepared by the cook, diners usually manage to eat a few extra calories.

Dishes not included in the book as recipes or variations are marked with an asterisk*. Ingredients for these and other specialities are obtainable from larger supermarkets or delicatessens specializing in French products.

Quick and easy lunch menus

Wine-growers' salad *(Salade des vignerons)*	41
Auvergne-style poached trout	
(Truite au bleu à la St-Roch)	60
Cherries in pancake batter *(Clafoutis)* (variation)	131
Salad with blue cheese dressing	
(Salade au Bresse bleu)	117
Fillet steak with mustard sauce *(Tournedos Dijonnaise)*	74
Pears in nut batter *(Flognarde aux poires et aux noix)*	
(variation)	131

Easy supper menus

Cream of sorrel soup *(Soupe dauphinoise)* (made ahead)	49
Arbois-style pork chops *(Côte de porc à l'Arboisienne)*	81
Custard tart *(Tarte au goumeau)*	136
Onion soup with port *(Gratinée Lyonnaise)* (variation)	50
Fillet steak with Roquefort sauce	
(Tournedos sauce Roquefort) (variation)	74
Frothy wine dessert *(Sabayon au vin)*	
(Using sweet wine or liqueur instead of champagne)	124

Menus to prepare in advance for entertaining

Chicken liver pâté *(Gâteau de foies de volaille)*	34
Vegetable soup with cheese toasts *(Soupe au Beaufort)*	
(the soup sieved and reheated)	51
Chicken poached with truffles *(Poularde demi-deuil)*	100
Cheese and walnut cream *(Crème de fromage aux noix)*	117
Grenoble walnut sponge cake *(Gâteau grenoblois)*	136
Truffle-stuffed goose neck *(Cou de l'oie farci aux truffes)*	35
Beef braised in red wine *(Bœuf bourguignon)*	68
Cheese with raisins *(Fromage aux raisins)*	117
Sponge cake with cinnamon pears	
(Biscuit de Savoie aux poires)	131

Regional menus

Alsace

Alsatian pizza *(Flammekueche)*	33
Meat and vegetable casserole *(Baeckeoffe)*	70
Munster cheese, served with Gewürztraminer*	—
Pear parfait in a kugelhopf mould	
(Kouglhopf glace Williams)	132

Lorraine

Bacon and egg quiche *(Quiche Lorraine)*	33
Stewed fish Lorraine style *(Matelote à la Lorraine)*	
(variation)	59
Munster-Géromé cheese*	—
Yeast cake with kirsch *(Baba au kirsch)*	122

Champagne

Wine-growers' salad *(Salade des vignerons)*	41
Trout in champagne *(Truites au champagne)*	62
Celeriac purée *(Purée de céleri)* (variation)	108
Chaource cheese served with Champagne*	—
Frothy champagne dessert *(Sabayon au champagne)*	124

Burgundy

Snails with garlic butter *(Escargots aux beurre d'ail)*	42
Leg of lamb in Burgundy wine *(Gigot d'agneau)* (variation)	90
Cheese with raisins *(Fromage aux raisins)*	117

Franche-Comté

Cheese toasts *(Croûte au Comté)*	29
Arbois-style pork chops *(Côte de porc à l'Arboisienne)*	81
Jura soft cheese *(Cancoillotte)*	118
Pancakes with fruit filling *(Matefaim)*	129

Bresse

Warm chicken liver pâté *(Gâteau de foies blonds)*	45
Bresse chicken in cream sauce	
(Poulet de Bresse à la crème)	99
Salad with blue cheese dressing *(Salade au Bresse bleu)*	117
Cheesecake with fruit sauce *(Gâteau au fromage blanc)*	128

Savoy

Prunes wrapped in bacon *(Pruneaux au Beaufort)*   28
Pumpkin soup with a puff pastry crust
  (Soupe de potiron en croûte)   53
Char with mushroom sauce *(Poisson à l'ancienne)*   56
Fermented cheese *(Fromage fort)*
  (made with Beaufort instead of Comté)   118
Sponge cake with cinnamon pears
  (Biscuit de Savoie aux poires)   131

Dauphiné

Cream of sorrel soup *(Soupe dauphinoise)*   49
Chicken with crayfish *(Poulet aux écrevisses)*   97
Cheese pâté *(Pétafine)*   118
Grenoble walnut sponge cake *(Gâteau grenoblois)*   136

Lyonnais

Chicken liver pâté *(Gâteau de foies de volaille)*   34
Pike dumplings *(Quenelles de brochet)*   44
Chicken with creamy vinegar sauce
  (Poulet au vinaigre)   98
Curd cheese with herbs *(Cervelle de canut)*   114
Lyonnais doughnuts *(Bugnes de Lyon)*   134

Auvergne

Cheese and mushroom flan *(Tarte aux champignons)*   30
Pigeons with green lentils *(Pigeonneau aux lentilles)*   86
Cheese and walnut cream *(Crème de fromage aux noix)*   117
Pears in pancake batter *(Flognarde aux poires)*   131

Limousin

Chestnut soup *(Potage aux châtaignes)*   49
Poached trout *(Truite au bleu)*
  (with melted butter instead of *Sauce à la St.-Roch*)   60
Tomme de Brach ewe's milk cheese*   —
Cherries in pancake batter *(Clafoutis)* (variation)   131

Seasonal menus

Spring menu

Bresse-style chicken salad *(Salade à la Bressane)*   38
Chicken with Jura wine *(Poulet au vin jaune)*   94
Creamed potatoes *(Purée de pommes de terre)*   108
Curd cheese with herbs *(Cervelle de canut)*   114
Cheesecake with fruit sauce
  (Gâteau au fromage blanc)   128

Summer menu

Ham in parsley aspic *(Jambon persillé)*   42
Auvergne-style poached trout
  (Truite au bleu à la St-Roch)   60
Lamb's brains in red wine sauce
  (Cervelle d'agneau meurette)   80
Cheese pâté *(Pétafine)*   118
Pear parfait in a kugelhopf mould
  (Kouglhopf glace Williams)   132

Autumn menu

Chestnut soup *(Potage aux châtaignes)*   49
Partridge with Puy lentils
  (Estouffade de perdrix aux lentilles du Puy)
  (variation)   86
Cheese and walnut cream
  (Crème de fromage aux noix)   117
Grenoble walnut sponge cake *(Gâteau grenoblois)*   136

Winter menu

Chicken dumplings with creamed lentils
  (Quenelles de volaille)   46
Carp stewed in red wine *(Meurette de carpes)*
  (variation)   64
Medallions of venison with cranberry sauce
  (Médaillon de biche)   89
Cheese with raisins *(Fromage aux raisins)*   117
"Snow eggs" *(Œufs à la neige)*   127

Festive menus

Easter

Bresse-style chicken salad *(Salade à la Bressane)*   38
Fish and white wine stew *(Pauchouse borguignonne)*   64
Seven-hour leg of mutton *(Gigot à la sept heures)*
  (variation)   70
Braised savoy cabbage *(Chou braisé)*   107
Cheese pâté *(Pétafine)*
Pancakes with fruit filling *(Matefaim)*   129
Coffee* and mini-doughnuts *(Café et Bugnes)*
  (variation)   134

Christmas

Oysters and pâté de foie gras*   —
Stuffed turkey *(Dinde farcie)* (variation)   92
Braised savoy cabbage with apples, prunes and
  chestnuts *(Chou braisé aux pommes, aux*
  pruneaux et aux châtaignes) (variation)   107
Chestnut purée *(Purée de châtaignes)*   104
Mont d'or (Vacherin cheese from the French Jura)*   —
Christmas log *(Bûche de Noel)** or Grenoble walnut
  sponge cake *(Gâteau grenoblois)*, made as a
  Christmas log. Spread the cake batter on a
  baking sheet and bake until golden. While still
  warm, roll up the sponge with a clean tea cloth,
  then leave to cool. Unroll, spread with the filling,
  then roll up again.   136
Coffee with chocolate truffles *(Café et truffes)*   133

New Year's Day

Oysters and pâté de foie gras*   —
Royal roast venison *(Rôti de chevreuil à la royale)*   90
Chestnut purée *(Purée de châtaignes)*   104
Cheese and walnut cream
  (Crème de fromage aux noix)   117
Champagne cream *(Crème champenoise)* (variation)   124

Glossary

This glossary is intended as a brief guide to some less familiar cookery terms and ingredients, including words and items found on menus in eastern France.

Aligot: creamed potatoes mixed with 24-hour-old *Tomme de Laguiole fraîche* (unfermented Cantal cheese), a speciality of the Auvergne.

Alsacienne, à l': name for dishes prepared Alsatian style, often with foie gras, sauerkraut and sausages.

AOC Appellation d'Origine Contrôlée: official certificate of quality and origin, applied to certain types of wine, poultry, fruit and cheese. The authorities granting the certificate strictly regulate the exact composition and combination of ingredients, as well as the growing or breeding conditions, and manufacturing processes and techniques.

Bain-marie: sweet and savoury sauces containing butter, eggs and cream easily curdle or burn if exposed to high heat. For this reason, they are prepared in a bain-marie or water bath. The vessel containing the sauce is suspended over a pan of hot water. Delicate dishes baked in the oven are placed in a roasting pan filled with enough boiling water to come halfway up the baking dish.

Beaufort: cow's milk cheese weighing up to 60 kg, with a concave top, produced in the alpine pastures of Savoy. This creamy, buttery cheese with its slightly cracked texture has a nutty flavour with hints of wild alpine flowers. It is left to mature for up to two years in cool, damp cellars.

Béchamel sauce: basic white sauce made from butter, flour and milk, seasoned with bay leaf, salt, pepper and nutmeg. *See also recipe, page 81.*

Blanch: to cook vegetables briefly in boiling water, drain, then plunge immediately into water chilled with ice cubes. This halts the cooking process and conserves the colour of the vegetables.

Bleu d'Auvergne: one of the best known French blue cheeses. *See also page 30.*

Blind-baking: a technique for baking unfilled pastry cases for flans or quiches to ensure thorough cooking. The pastry base is pricked all over with a fork, lined with greaseproof paper and weighted with dry beans or peas. It is baked for 10 to 15 minutes; then the beans and paper are removed and the filling added for cooking.

Bouillon: stock made from either fish bones and scraps, poultry giblets, or stewing meat and bones, boiled with wine, water, vegetables and seasonings, then strained and skimmed. Vegetable stock is made simply with a mixture of different vegetables.

Bouquet garni: a bundle of several herbs—the classic three are bay leaf, thyme and parsley—tied together and used to flavour a stock or stew. The bouquet garni is removed and discarded at the end of the cooking time.

Bourguignonne, à la: literally "Burgundy style", a name for dishes prepared with red wine, cognac, bacon, mushrooms and small onions.

Bresse chickens: free-range poultry excellent enough to carry the AOC. *See also page 94.*

Brillat-Savarin: famous gastronome who lived from 1755 to 1826. The creamy cow's milk cheese is named after him.

Brioche: light yeast cake made with lots of butter and egg.

Bugnes: a type of doughnut traditionally eaten during Lent in the Lyon area. *See also Note, page 134.*

Cancoillotte: soft cheese made from *metton* (curdled skimmed milk), white wine, butter and garlic, a Franche-Comté speciality. *See also page 118.*

Cantal: cylindrical cheese weighing up to 50 kg, made from raw cow's milk, with a flavour of wild flowers and mountain herbs. Produced in the Auvergne between May and September, when the most milk is produced, by dairymen who spend the season with the cattle, living in *burons* (stone-built alpine huts). The cheese matures in the *burons* for at least four months. The Cantal-Laguiole cheese sold in the markets of the region is matured for up to two years.

Cassis: blackcurrant used to make crème de cassis.

Cassis, crème de: blackcurrant liqueur.

Charolais cattle: popular breed of beef cattle. *See also page 75.*

Châtaigne: sweet chestnuts. *See also page 105.*

Court bouillon: aromatic stock used in preparation of fish and meat dishes.

Crème anglaise: custard made with egg, milk, sugar and vanilla, whisked in a bain-marie until creamy.

Crème fraîche: a slightly ripened, sharp-tasting French double cream containing about 35 per cent fat.

Croûtons: small cubes of bread, toasted or fried in fat, used as a garnish for soup.

Daubière: earthenware pot, glazed on the inside, used for slow cooking.

Deglazing: after food has been sautéed and the food and excess fat removed from the pan, a small amount of liquid, such as wine, is heated in the pan, and stirred well to loosen food stuck to the bottom. The deglazing juices can be added to sauces or stocks.

Demi-deuil: literally "half-mourning", a preparation method in which slices of black truffles are inserted under the skin of a chicken, or other poultry. *See also recipe, page 100.*

Diots: small pork sausages, made only in the Savoy countryside, usually boiled in white wine.

Eau-de-vie: distilled wine or clear spirit distilled from fruit or grain.

Flambé: spirit with an alcohol content of at least 38 per cent is warmed in a ladle then poured over meat and ignited. The alcohol burns away, leaving its flavour.

Fond: pan juices used as a base for making sauces.

Ile flottante: literally "floating island", another name for *Oeufs à la neige*. *See also page 127.*

Kugelhopf, kouglhopf, kougelhof, kouglof: ring-shaped yeast pound-cake, with raisins and almonds, a speciality of the Alsace region. *See also recipe, page 132.*

Lyonnaise, à la: literally "in the style of Lyon", a name given to certain dishes prepared with onions.

Marc: a potent brandy distilled from the residue of grapes after pressing. It is a popular drink in France.

Matelote: freshwater fish stewed in red or white wine.

Meurette: Red wine sauce or fish stewed in red wine.

Pain de mie: dense sandwich loaf with very little crust. Unlike most types of French bread, it is made with milk, sugar and butter.

Pain viennois: baguette-shaped white loaf made with milk, white flour, sugar and yeast.

Parfait: partly-frozen cream dessert made with eggs, whipped cream and fruit. Duck, goose and chicken liver mousse is also known as *parfait.*

Plucking roses: a technical culinary term for testing custard or a sauce made with egg yolk. Dip a wooden spoon in the custard and blow on the custard clinging to the spoon. If it forms a rose shape and does not run off the wooden spoon, the consistency is right. Alternatively, test the custard by seeing if it will coat the back of a wooden spoon.

Potage: thick soup, usually made with vegetables.

Pot-au-feu: literally "pot on the fire", a meat and vegetable stew, served as two courses, first broth, then meat and vegetables. *See also recipe, page 73.*

Potée: savoury hotpot, usually made with pork and regional vegetables—in eastern France, mainly cabbage and potatoes.

Puy lentils: greeny-blue lentils from Le Puy in the Auvergne, smaller than other green or brown lentils, with a particularly good flavour. *See also page 46.*

Ratafia: in France, ratafia is a fruit brandy made from grape juice. In Britain, Victorian cookery books were full of recipes for different ratafias—now largely forgotten—made from various fruits, brandy and bitter almonds. Nowadays ratafia more commonly refers to a small, sweet, almond-flavoured biscuit.

Reinette: a sweet apple used for cooking in France.

Salers: semi-hard cow's milk cheese, very similar to Cantal, produced in the *burons* (alpine huts in the Auvergne) during the summer months of May to September.

Saucisse de Strasbourg: red-skinned sausage similar to a frankfurter.

Saucisson de Lyon: air-dried sausage made with lean pork and beef, bacon and garlic, often containing truffles.

Skim: to remove the fat from soups and sauces after cooking. This can be done with a spoon or ladle, or paper towel can be pulled across the layer of fat. You can also let the liquid cool (this is quickly done if the saucepan is placed in a larger pan of water with ice cubes in it) and then left in the refrigerator. The fat will then set on the top and be firm enough to be removed with a spoon.

Testing: to test whether a cake is done, insert a fine skewer into the centre. If it comes out clean and dry, the cake is cooked. Poultry should be tested by pricking the thickest part of the leg with a fine skewer. The juice will run clear if the meat is cooked through. Test vegetables and stews by tasting a small piece. Where a gelling agent is being used, such as in jelly or aspic, place a tablespoonful of the mixture on a small, cold plate. Leave in the refrigerator for a few minutes, then test to see whether it is sufficiently set or whether more gelatine is needed.

Truffles: the world's most expensive fungus, unearthed by specially trained truffle hounds or pigs. Black truffles have a more refined flavour than the white variety. The liquid in which truffles are preserved is known as truffle juice. The term truffle is also used for soft, round chocolate sweets. *See also recipe, page 133.*

Verjus: verjuice, the juice of unripe grapes. It gives a sour, piquant flavour to food. *See also Note, page 41.*

Vinaigrette: salad dressing made with vinegar, mustard, seasonings and oil.

Vin jaune: Jura's one famous wine, a sherry-like yellow wine, which derives its colour from maturing in oak for six years. To conserve its nutty bouquet, it is served at room temperature in brandy glasses.

Whitefish: not to be confused with "white fish" (two words), denoting cod, haddock etc., whitefish is a mackerel-like freshwater fish found in the deep cold lakes of the Northern hemisphere.

CONVERSION CHART

These figures are not exact equivalents, but have been rounded up or down slightly to make measuring easier.

Weight Equivalents		Volume Equivalents	
Metric	Imperial	Metric	Imperial
15 g	½ oz	8 cl	3 fl oz
30 g	1 oz	12.5 cl	4 fl oz
60 g	2 oz	15 cl	¼ pint
90 g	3 oz	17.5 cl	6 fl oz
125 g	¼ lb	25 cl	8 fl oz
150 g	5 oz	30 cl	½ pint
200 g	7 oz	35 cl	12 fl oz
250 g	½ lb	45 cl	¾ pint
350 g	¾ lb	50 cl	16 fl oz
500 g	1 lb	60 cl	1 pint
1 kg	2 to 2¼ lb	1 litre	35 fl oz

Recipe Index

Aligo 108
Almonds, whitefish with, 63
Alsatian:
    goose 93
    pizza 33
    yeast cake (variation) 123
Arbois-style pork chops 81
Aspic, ham in parsley, 42
Auvergne-style poached trout 60

Baba au kirsch 122
Bacon:
    and egg quiche 33
    potato cake with, and Cantal cheese
    (variation) 76
    prunes wrapped in, 28
Baeckeoffe 70
Beef:
    boiled, with vegetables and
    coarse salt 73
    braised in red wine 68
    stock (Note) 53
Biscuit de Savoie aux poires 131
Bleu d'Auvergne 30
Bœuf bourguignon 68
Bresse chicken in cream sauce 99
Bresse chickens 94
Bresse-style chicken salad 38
Bugnes (variation) 134
Bugnes de Lyon 134
Burgundy wine, leg of lamb in, (variation)
    90

Cabbage, savoy, braised, 107
    with apples, prunes and chestnuts
    (variation) 107
Cancoillotte 118
Cantal cheese, potato cake with bacon
    and, (variation) 76
Carp stewed in red wine (variation) 64
Celeriac purée (variation) 108
Cervelle d'agneau meurette 80
Cervelle de canut 114
Champagne: 124
    cream (variation) 124
    dessert, frothy, 124
    trout in, 62
Char with mushroom sauce 56
Charolais cattle 75
Cheese:
    blue, dressing, salad with, 117
    creamed potatoes with, 108
    fermented, 118
    Jura soft, 118
    and mushroom flan 30
    onion soup with, 50
    and potato soufflé 118
    with raisins 117
    toasts 29
    vegetable soup with, 51
    and walnut cream 117

Cheesecake with fruit sauce 128
Cherries in pancake batter (variation)
    131
Chestnut:
    purée 104
    soup 49
Chestnuts, sweet, 105
Chicken:
    Bresse, in cream sauce 99
    with crayfish 97
    with creamy vinegar sauce 98
    with Jura wine 94
    liver pâté 34; warm, 45
    poached with truffles 100
    salad, Bresse-style, 38
    stock (Note) 38
Chickens, Bresse, 94
Chocolate truffles 133
Chou braisé 107
Chou braisé aux pommes, aux pruneaux
    et aux châtaignes (variation) 107
Choucroute à l'Alsacienne 107
Choucroute garnie à l'Alsacienne
    (variation) 107
Clafoutis (variation) 131
Côte de porc à l'Arboisienne 81
Cou de l'oie farci aux truffes 35
Cranberry sauce, medallions of venison
    with, 89
Crayfish, chicken with, 97
Cream: 115
    sauce; Bresse chicken in, 99;
    tripe in vinegar and, 82
    trout cooked in red wine and, 59
Crème champenoise (variation) 124
Crème de fromage aux noix 117
Croûte au Beaufort 29
Curd cheese with herbs 114
Custart tart 136

Dinde farcie (variation) 92
Dinde rôtie 92
Doughnuts:
    Lyonnais, 134
    mini (variation) 134
Dumplings, pike, 44

Egg quiche, bacon and, 33
Eggs: 60
    "Snow" 127
Escalopes de chevreuil au gratin
    dauphinois (variation) 89
Escargots aux beurre d'ail 42
Estouffade de perdrix aux lentilles du Puy
    (variation) 86

Féras aux amandes 63
Fish:
    stewed, Lorraine style (variation) 59
    stock (Note) 59
    and white wine stew 64

Flammekueche 33
Flognarde aux poires131
Flognarde aux poires et aux noix
    (variation) 131
Fromage aux raisins 117
Fromage fort 118
Fruit:
    filling, pancakes with, 129
    sauce, cheesecake with, 128

Garlic butter, snails with, 42
Gâteau au fromage blanc 128
Gâteau de foies blondes 45
Gâteau de foies de volaille 34
Gâteau grenoblois 136
Gigot à la sept heures (variation) 70
Gigot brayaude 70
Gigot d'agneau (variation) 90
Goose:
    neck, truffle-stuffed, 35
    Alsatian, 93
Grape-pickers' stew 73
Gras-double comtoise 82
Gratin savoyard et diots 79
Gratinée Lyonnaise (variation) 50
Grenoble walnut sponge cake 136
Grenoble-style trout (variation) 63

Ham in parsley aspic 42
Herbs, curd cheese with, 114
Herring salad from Lyon 41

Jambon persillé 42
Jura:
    soft cheese 118
    wine, chicken with, 94

Kirsch, yeast cake with, 122
Kouglhopf glace Williams 132
Kugelhopf (variation) 123

Lamb's brains in red wine sauce 80
Lamb, leg of:
    in Burgundy wine (variation) 90
    pot-roasted, 70
    seven hour, (variation) 70
Lentils:
    pigeons with green, 86
    Puy, 46
Lorraine style, stewed fish, (variation)
    59

Matefaim 129
Matelote à la Lorraine (variation)
    59
Matelote de truite 59
Meat and vegetable casserole 70
Médaillon de biche 89
Meurette de carpes (variation) 64
Mini-doughnuts (variation) 134
Morel sauce, tripe in, (variation) 82

Mushroom:
   flan, cheese and, 30
   sauce, char with, 56
Mustard sauce, fillet steak with, 74

Nut batter, pears in (variation) 131

Oeufs à la neige 127
Oie à l'Alsacienne 93
Onion soup:
   with cheese 50
   with port (variation) 50

Pancake batter:
   pears in, 131
   cherries in, (variation) 131
Pancakes with fruit filling 129
Parfait, pear, in a kugelhopf mould 132
Partridge with Puy lentils (variation) 86
Pâté:
   cheese, 118
   chicken liver, 34; warm, 45
Pauchouse bourguignonne 64
Pear parfait in a kugelhopf mould 132
Pears:
   in nut batter (variation) 131
   in pancake batter 131
   sponge cake with cinnamon, 131
Pétafine 118
Pigeonneau aux lentilles 86
Pigeons with green lentils 86
Pike dumplings 44
Pizza, Alsation, 33
Poisson à l'ancienne 56
Pommes de terre lyonnaise 111
Pork:
   chops, Arbois-style, 81
   sausage (variation) 76
Port, onion soup with, (variation) 50
Pot-au-feu de boeuf gros sel 73
Pot-roasted leg of lamb 70
Potage aux châtaignes 49
Potato:
   cake with bacon and Cantal cheese
   (variation) 76
   and cheese soufflé 110
   gratin with sausages in wine sauce 79;
   escalopes of venison with, (variation)
   89
   salad, hot sausages with, 79
Potatoes:
   creamed, 108; with cheese 108
   sauté, with onions 111
Potée des vendangeurs 73
Poularde demi-deuil 100
Poulet au vin jaune 94
Poulet au vinaigre 98
Poulet aux écrevisses 97
Poulet de Bresse à la crème 99
Pountari (variation) 76
Pounti 76

Pruneaux au Beaufort 28
Prunes wrapped in bacon 28
Pumpkin soup with a puff pastry crust 53
Pureé de céleri (variation) 108
Pureé de châtaignes 104
Pureé de pommes de terre 108
Puy lentils: 46
   partridge with, (variation) 86

Quenelles de brochet 44
Quenelles de volaille 46
Quiche Lorraine 33

Raisins, cheese with, 117
Roquefort sauce, fillet steak with,
   (variation) 74
Rôti de chevreui là la royale 90

Sabayon au champagne 124
Salad:
   with blue cheese dressing 117
   Bresse-style chicken, 38
   herring, from Lyon, 41
   wine-growers, 41
Salade à la Bressane 38
Salade à la Lyonnaise 41
Salade au Bresse bleu 117
Salade des vignerons 41
Saucisson, pommes à l'huile 79
Sauerkraut, Alsace, 107;
   garnished with mixed meat and
   sausages (variation) 107
Sausage, pork, (variation) 76
Sausages:
   hot, with potato salad 79
   potato gratin with, in wine sauce 79
Sauté potatoes with onions 111
Seven-hour leg of lamb (variation) 70
Snails with garlic butter 42
"Snow eggs" 127
Sorrel soup, cream of, 49
Soufflé de pommes de terre 110
Soup:
   chestnut, 49
   cream of sorrel, 49
   pumpkin, with a puff pastry crust 53
   vegetable, with cheese toasts, 51
Soupe au Beaufort 51
Soupe au Cantal 50
Soupe dauphinoise 49
Soupe de potiron en croûte 53
Sponge cake with cinnamon pears 131
Steak, fillet:
   with mustard sauce 74
   with Roquefort sauce (variation) 74
Stew, grape-pickers', 73
Stock:
   beef (Note) page 53
   chicken (Note) page 38;
Sweet chestnuts 105
Swiss chard pudding 76

Tart, custard, 136
Tarte au goumeau 136
Tarte aux champignons 30
Tournedos Dijonnaise 74
Tournedos sauce Roquefort, (variation)
   74
Tripe:
   in morel sauce (variation) 82
   in vinegar and cream sauce 82
Tripes aux morilles (variation) 82
Trout:
   Auvergne-style poached, 60
   in champagne 62
   cooked in red wine and cream 59
   Grenoble-style, (variation) 63
Truffado, (variation) 76
Truffes 133
Truffle-stuffed goose neck 35
Truffles:
   chicken poached with, 100
   chocolate, 133
Truite au bleu à la St.-Roch 60
Truites au champagne 62
Truites grenobloises, (variation) 63
Turkey:
   roast, 92
   stuffed, (variation) 92

Vegetable:
   casserole, meat and, 70
   soup with cheese toasts 51
Vegetables with coarse salt, boiled beef
   and, 73
Venison:
   escalopes of, with potato gratin
   (variation) 89
   medallions of, with cranberry sauce
   89
   royal roast, 90
Vinegar:
   and cream sauce, tripe in, 82
   sauce, chicken with creamy, 98

Walnut:
   cream, cheese and, 117
   sponge cake, Grenoble, 136
Whitefish with almonds 63
Wine:
   sauce, potato gratin with sausages
   in, 79
   Jura, chicken with, 94
   red, and cream, trout cooked in, 59
   beef braised in, 68
   carp stewed in, (variation) 64
   sauce, lamb's brains in, 80
   white, stew, fish and, 64
Wine-growers' salad 41

Yeast cake:
   Alsation, (variation) 123
   with kirsch 122

Cover: A classic dish of the region, Quiche Lorraine *(recipe, page 33)* is best served warm, but is also delicious cold. Once the pastry has been prepared, quiche is very easy to cook and only requires a few ingredients—eggs, milk, cream and bacon, plus a little seasoning. It can be served in the form of separate tartlets for a cocktail snack (as in the picture) or as a single, larger tart for a light meal accompanied by salad and a white wine.

TIME-LIFE BOOKS

COOKERY AROUND THE WORLD
English edition staff for *France: The East*
Editorial: Christine Noble, Felicity Jackson, Kate Cann, Mark Stephenson
Designer: Dawn McGinn
Production: Emma Wishart, Justina Cox
Technical Consultant: Michael A. Barnes

English translation by Isabel Varea for Ros Schwartz Translations, London

Produced by Gräfe und Unzer Verlag GmbH, Munich
© 1995 Gräfe und Unzer Verlag GmbH, Munich

This edition published by Time-Life Books B.V. Amsterdam
Authorized English language edition
© 1995 Time-Life Books B.V.
First English language printing 1995

TIME-LIFE is a trademark of Time Warner Inc. U.S.A.

ISBN 0 7054 3520 2

Colour reproduction by Fotolito Longo, Bolzano, Italy
Output by Leaside Graphics, Luton, England
Printed and bound by Mondadori, Verona, Italy

GRÄFE UND UNZER

EDITOR: Dr Stephanie von Werz-Kovacs
Editor-in-Chief: Petra Bachmann
Designer: Konstantin Kern
Production: VerlagsService Dr. Helmut Neuberger & Karl Schaumann GmbH, Heimstetten
Recipes tested by: Traute Hatterscheid, Dorothea Henghuber, Christa Konrad-Seiter, Marianne Obermayr
Cartography: Huber

Amandine Ditta Biegi was born in Dresden and now lives in Nice. Her enthusiasm for French cuisine has led her to attend a number of cookery seminars and she has also taken lessons from a top French chef. In the course of her many gastronomic tours around France and whilst working on her own cookery page for a newspaper in the south of France, Amandine has amassed an extensive collection of authentic regional recipes. A selection of those from eastern France and the Massif Central appear in this book. She has won a number of prizes for traditional and creative French cuisine.

Michael Brauner, is a graduate of the Berlin Fotoschule. He worked as an assistant to several French and German photographers and specialized in food photography for five years before setting up on his own in 1984. He now divides his time between his studios in Karlsruhe and Gordes in Provence.

Kathrin Gaus was born in Braunschweig where she studied graphic design. She now lives in the south of France and her affection for the area is shown clearly in her illustrations.

Picture Credits

Colour illustrations: Kathrin Gaus

All photographs by Michael Brauner, Food Fotografie, unless indicated below:

Cover: Graham Kirk, London. 4-5 top (chickens and ducks on a farm at Montreval-en-Bresse), centre left (Ferme Musée de la Fôret, a farming museum in Saint-Trivier-de-Courtes), bottom left (a bar in Lyon): Amandine Ditta Biegl, Nice; centre right (St Stephen's Cathedral, Metz), bottom right (a grape-picker in Burgundy): Martin Thomas, Aix-la-Chapelle. 8-9: Lothar Schiffler/AV-Bilderbank, Munich. 10, 11 top: Martin Thomas, Aix-la-Chapelle. 11 bottom: Marika Windisch/Silvestris Fotoservice, Kastl. 12 top, 13 top: Martin Siepmann/Silvestris Fotoservice, Kastl. 12 bottom, 13 bottom: Dietlind Castor, Lindau. 14: Christian Heeb. 15 top: Martin Thomas, Aix-la-Chapelle. 15 bottom: Thomas Stankiewicz, Munich. 16: Amandine Ditta Biegl, Nice. 17: Lothar Schiffler/AV-Bilderbank, Munich. 18: Werner Richner, Saarlouis. 19: Martin Thomas, Aix-la-Chapelle. 20: Andreas Riedmiller, Oberzollhaus. 21 top: Aldo Acquardo/Agentur Look, Munich. 21 bottom: Amandine Ditta Biegl, Nice. 22, 23 top: Martin Thomas, Aix-la-Chapelle. 23 bottom: Werner Richner, Saarlouis. 24: Amandine Ditta Biegl, Nice. 25: Lothar Schiffler/AV-Bilderbank, Munich. 75, 94: Amandine Ditta Biegl, Nice. 105: Martin Thomas, Aix-la-Chapelle. 124: Hermann Rademacker, Munich.

Acknowledgement

Special thanks to the "Fondation Auguste Escoffier" for allowing Amandine Ditta Biegi to use their library in her research.